God and Evidence

God and Evidence

Problems for Theistic Philosophers

Rob Lovering

B L O O M S B U R Y

NEW YORK · LONDON · NEW DELHI · SYDNEY

Bloomsbury Academic
An imprint of Bloomsbury Publishing Inc

1385 Broadway	50 Bedford Square
New York	London
NY 10018	WC1B 3DP
USA	UK

www.bloomsbury.com

Bloomsbury is a registered trade mark of Bloomsbury Publishing Plc

First published 2013
Paperback edition first published 2014

© Rob Lovering, 2013

Library of Congress Cataloging-in-Publication Data
Lovering, Rob.
God and evidence: problems for theistic philosophers/Rob Lovering.
pages cm
Includes bibliographical references and index.
ISBN 978-1-4411-4943-5 (alk. paper)
1. Theism. 2. God. I. Title.
BL200.L68 2013
211'.3–dc23
2012049949

ISBN: HB: 978-1-4411-4943-5
       PB: 978-1-6289-2807-5
       ePub: 978-1-6235-6146-8
       ePDF: 978-1-6235-6960-0

Typeset by Deanta Global Publishing Services, Chennai, India

Contents

Acknowledgments

This book draws from a number of my articles. Accordingly, I would like to thank the following journals for allowing me to use material from those articles—*International Journal for Philosophy of Religion* ("Divine Hiddenness and Inculpable Ignorance," Vol. 56, Nos. 2–3 (2004): 89–107, and "On What God Would Do," Vol. 66, No. 2 (2009): 87–104; *Philo* ("The Problem of the Theistic Evidentialist Philosophers," Vol. 13, No. 2 (2010): 185–200); *Sophia* ("On the Morality of Having Faith that God Exists," Vol. 51, No. 1 (April 2012): 17–30); and *Religious Studies* ("Does God Know What It is Like Not to Know?", Vol. 49, No. 1 (2013):85–99).

A special thanks goes to Paul Studtmann. Not only did Paul recommend that I write this book, he read a draft of it and provided very helpful comments. Indeed, whenever I needed to discuss the book with another philosopher, Paul was my go-to-guy, and his comments were consistently useful.

Another special thanks goes to my wife, Lucia. From the beginning, Lucia patiently listened as I updated her on each new development, no matter how trivial the development might have been. Her love and encouragement has been, and continues to be, invaluable to me.

Finally, I dedicate this book to Ed. L. Miller, who took a chance on an underprepared but ambitious graduate student. Without his belief in me and subsequent support, it is safe to say that this book never would have been written. Thanks, Ed.

1

Introduction

Introduction

For nearly two millennia, theistic philosophers have had to contend with problems raised against their theistic beliefs. Typically raised by nontheistic (atheistic and agnostic) philosophers, these problems have ranged from critiques of theistic philosophers' arguments for God's existence to arguments for the nonexistence of God.

In this book, I present a new set of problems for theistic philosophers' theistic beliefs. The problems pertain specifically to three types of theistic philosopher, to be referred to here as "theistic inferentialists," "theistic noninferentialists," and "theistic fideists" (to be defined shortly). Each type of theistic philosopher faces a problem unique to his or her type, and they all share two problems, or so I shall argue. In some cases, the problems raised here take us down an entirely new discursive path; in others, they take us down a new discursive path branching off from an old one. In every case, however, they are paths that take us further and further away from theism.

The purpose of this chapter is to provide you with the backdrop against which the rest of the book is to be understood and evaluated. Specifically, in this chapter, I address a number of important concepts and distinctions as well as briefly present the problems to be raised against the theistic beliefs of these three types of theistic philosopher. I begin, however, with an observation about the current philosophical debate over theism.

Theism: A philosophical Alamo

It is not uncommon for the debate between theistic philosophers and their nontheistic counterparts to be described in terms of a battle. Augustine of Hippo, for example, describes it as a battle between the *civitas Dei* (the city of God) and the *civitas mundi* (the city of the world).[1] I, too, am inclined to describe the debate between theistic philosophers and their nontheistic counterparts in terms of a battle—for it reminds me of a particular historical battle, the Battle of the Alamo.

As many of us learned in grade school, there was a significant disparity of numbers between the defenders of the Alamo and their adversaries, the former being outnumbered

---

[1] Augustine of Hippo (1994), *The City of God*, trans. Marcus Dods. New York, NY: The Modern Library.

by the latter roughly 5,500 to 260. In this respect, the Battle of the Alamo reminds me of the battle between theistic philosophers and their nontheistic counterparts. You see, according to a recent survey of 931 philosophy faculty members, 15 percent accept or lean toward theism, 73 percent accept or lean toward atheism, and the rest accept or lean toward the "other" category (of which, some undoubtedly accept or lean toward agnosticism).[2] Since accepting or leaning toward atheism or "other" involves not accepting or leaning toward theism, an overwhelming 85 percent of these philosophy faculty members do not accept or lean toward theism. These statistics suggest that, in the world of professional philosophy, theistic philosophers occupy a role similar to that of the defenders of the Alamo, one in which they are significantly outnumbered by their adversaries, but steadfast in their convictions nonetheless. (This is not to suggest, of course, that theistic philosophers are the "good guys" and nontheistic philosophers are the "bad guys," or vice versa. The metaphor only goes so far.)

With the preceding in mind, a question naturally arises—whence the great statistical disparity between theistic and nontheistic philosophers? Theistic, atheistic, and agnostic philosophers must have their reasons for being theistic, atheistic, and agnostic philosophers (respectively). But, what are they? More specifically, what *kinds* of reasons are they? Are they evidential reasons—reasons that indicate the truth of their theistic, atheistic, and agnostic beliefs? Are they nonevidential reasons—reasons that induce their theistic, atheistic, and agnostic beliefs, but do not thereby indicate the truth of them? Are they both? There is virtually no doubt that the reasons they have for being theistic, atheistic, and agnostic philosophers are both evidential and nonevidential in nature. That this is the case for theistic philosophers in particular— the focus of this book—may be defended briefly as follows.

Regarding evidential reasons, some theistic philosophers are known for the evidential reasons they have provided for believing that God exists. From Thomas Aquinas and his "five ways" of proving God's existence to William Paley and his version of the teleological argument, to William Lane Craig and his version of the Kalām cosmological argument, to Richard Swinburne and his version of the argument from religious experience—these and other theistic philosophers are known for the evidential reasons they have provided for believing that God exists. And there is no doubt that these evidential reasons are among the reasons these and other theistic philosophers have for believing that God exists.

As for nonevidential reasons, some theistic philosophers are known for the nonevidential reasons they have provided for believing that God exists. From Blaise Pascal and his divine wager to Søren Kierkegaard and his leap of faith, to William James and his will to believe, to John Bishop and his supra-evidential fideism—these and other theistic philosophers are known for the nonevidential reasons they have provided for believing that God exists. And, as with the preceding evidential reasons, there is no doubt that these nonevidential reasons are among the reasons these and other theistic philosophers have for believing that God exists.

---

[2] http://philpapers.org/surveys/results.pl?affil=Target+faculty&areas0=0&areas_max=1&grain=coarse.

Much more will be said about the theistic philosophers' evidential and nonevidential reasons for believing that God exists in the chapters to come. For now, suffice it to say that the reasons theistic philosophers have for belief in God's existence fall into the following categories—evidential and nonevidential. Together, these reasons constitute the ammunition with which theistic philosophers have defended and continue to defend what appears to be a philosophical version of the Alamo—theism.

With these two categories in mind, another categorical division may be made, one pertaining to theistic philosophers themselves. Though each theistic philosopher to be addressed here believes that God exists, not all believe that discoverable probabilifying evidence of God's existence exists, be it inferential or noninferential evidence (to be explained shortly). In short, some of them believe that discoverable probabilifying evidence of God's existence exists, while others do not. Accordingly, these theistic philosophers may be divided into three categories, the first two of which include belief in discoverable probabilifying evidence of God's existence and the third of which does not:

1. Theistic inferentialists—philosophers who believe that (a) God exists, (b) there is inferential probabilifying evidence of God's existence, and (c) this evidence is discoverable not simply in principle, but in practice.
2. Theistic noninferentialists—philosophers who believe that (a) God exists, (b) there is noninferential probabilifying evidence of God's existence, and (c) this evidence is discoverable not simply in principle, but in practice.
3. Theistic fideists—philosophers who believe that (a) God exists, (b) there is no discoverable probabilifying evidence of God's existence, but (c) it is acceptable—morally, if not otherwise—to have faith that God exists.

The first two types of theistic philosopher are not to be understood as being mutually exclusive—one can be at once a theistic inferentialist and a theistic noninferentialist. However, the first two types of theistic philosopher, on the one hand, and the third type of theistic philosopher, on the other, *are* to be understood as being mutually exclusive—one cannot be a theistic inferentialist and/or theistic noninferentialist and, at the same time, a theistic fideist.

More will be said about each of these types of theistic philosopher in a moment. But before doing so, we must first analyze some of the preceding definitions' key concepts as well as a few others.

Key concepts

There are a number of key concepts, including:

- theism (along with its counterparts—atheism and agnosticism)
- theistic philosopher (along with its counterparts—atheistic philosopher and agnostic philosopher), and

- evidence (along with its various types—inferential, noninferential, public, private, probabilifying, and discoverable)

Each will be analyzed in turn.

Beginning with theism, it may be understood in either a broad or narrow sense.[3] For present purposes, by the broad sense of "theism," I mean the view that a god of one sort or another exists; while by the narrow sense of "theism," I mean the view that a particular god exists, namely, an omniscient, omnipotent, perfectly good, sovereign being who created the universe—in a word, "God." (Many other properties have been attributed to God, of course, but the preceding will suffice for now.)[4] God, according to the narrow sense of theism, is the greatest actual being, if not the greatest possible being, the only source of hesitation being whether a greatest possible being is indeed possible.[5]

Which sense of theism is at work in the survey mentioned above is not clear, for the survey does not indicate what exactly it means by "theism." As a result, some of the philosophers who accept or lean toward theism may do so only in the broad sense. (Those who accept or lean toward theism in the narrow sense do so in the broad sense as well, of course, since narrow theism implies broad theism.) That said, given that all of the theistic philosophers to be addressed in this book embrace theism in the narrow sense, theism will be understood hereafter in the narrow sense.

By "theistic philosopher," then, I mean a philosopher who believes that God exists. One can be a theistic philosopher without being formally trained in philosophy, let alone being a professional philosopher, such as a philosophy faculty member. That said, when I refer to theistic philosophers, I mean to refer specifically to those philosophers who are or were professional philosophers or who have or had enough philosophical training to be one. Examples of theistic philosophers abound—Augustine of Hippo, Anselm of Canterbury, Thomas Aquinas, William Paley, Blaise Pascal, Søren Kierkegaard, Alvin Plantinga, William Alston, Robin Collins, William Lane Craig, Stephen T. Davis, C. Stephen Layman, Marilyn McCord Adams, Nicolas Wolterstorff, and Linda Zagzebski, among others.

As with theism and theistic philosophers, there are broad and narrow senses of atheism and atheistic philosophers as well as agnosticism and agnostic philosophers. As with theism, each will be understood here in the narrow sense. Accordingly, by "atheism," I mean the view that God does not exist; and by "atheistic philosopher," I mean a philosopher who believes that God does not exist. By "agnosticism," I mean the view neither that God exists nor that God does not exist—in other words, the suspension of belief with regard to God's existence. And, by "agnostic philosopher," I

---

[3] The language of "broad" and "narrow" is borrowed from William Rowe. See William Rowe (2007), *Philosophy of Religion: An Introduction*, 4th edition. Belmont, CA: Wadsworth Publishing Company, 16.

[4] Other properties attributed to God include eternal, omnipresent, nonphysical, necessarily existing, simple, immutable, impassable, etc. See Nicholas Everitt (2010), "The Divine Attributes," *Philosophy Compass* 5: 78.

[5] Just as a greatest possible natural number is not possible, so a greatest possible being may not be possible.

mean a philosopher who neither believes that God exists nor believes that God does not exist.

Also, just as one can be a theistic philosopher without being a professional philosopher, so can one be an atheistic or agnostic philosopher without being a professional philosopher. That said, when I refer to atheistic and agnostic philosophers, I mean to refer specifically to those philosophers who are or were professional philosophers or who have or had enough philosophical training to be one. Examples of atheistic and agnostic philosophers abound as well—Baron d'Holbach, David Hume, Friedrich Nietzsche, Bertrand Russell, J. L. Mackie, Michael Tooley, William Rowe, Michael Martin, Philip Kitcher, Nicholas Everitt, J. L. Schellenberg, Daniel Dennett, Paul Draper, Graham Oppy, Richard Gale, and A. C. Grayling, among others.

By "evidence," I mean epistemic reasons—reasons that indicate the truth of beliefs. For example, if existence is a perfection (as some theistic philosophers maintain) and if God possesses all the perfections, then that existence is a perfection is an epistemic reason for believing that God exists—it indicates the truth of the belief that God exists. Epistemic reasons stand in contrast with nonepistemic reasons—reasons that induce beliefs, but do not thereby indicate their truth. An example of a nonepistemic reason for believing that God exists is a beneficial reason, a reason characterized by the benefits of so believing. Perhaps needless to say, that it is beneficial in one way or another to believe that God exists is not, in and of itself, an indication that the belief is true.[6]

Another thing to note about evidence—as it will be understood here, anyway—is that it may be public or private in nature. By "public" evidence of God's existence, I mean evidence that is objective and thereby "open to the awareness and inspection to anyone who is interested enough to consider" it, as Stephen Davis puts it.[7] In other words, public evidence is evidence that it is, in principle, possible for anyone to evaluate. Examples of public evidence of God's existence include philosophical arguments, scientific data, and testimony. By "private" evidence of God's existence, however, I mean evidence that is subjective and thereby open "only to the awareness and scrutiny of the given individual to whom [it is] private, and [is] not necessarily convincing to anyone else."[8] An individual-specific religious experience wherein God presents himself to the individual is an instance of private evidence of God's existence.[9]

---

[6] To be sure, true beliefs may confer benefits on those who assent to them, though arguably not in every case (e.g., it is not clear how assenting to the true belief "The number of biological organisms on Earth at this moment is odd or even" would be beneficial). But that it is beneficial to believe something is not, in and of itself, a reason to think that the belief itself is true. The relation between true beliefs and beneficial beliefs, then, is asymmetrical—true beliefs may as such confer benefits, but beneficial beliefs do not as such confer truth.

[7] Stephen T. Davis (1978), *Faith, Skepticism, and Evidence*. Cranbury, NJ: Associated University Presses, 26.

[8] Ibid., 28.

[9] It should be noted that not all philosophers agree that private evidence of this sort is possible. For example, Richard Swinburne thinks that it is, while Nicholas Everitt thinks that it is not. See Richard Swinburne (1979), *The Existence of God*. Oxford: Clarendon Press, 248; and Nicholas Everitt (2009), *The Non-existence of God*. London: Routledge, 161ff.

As for "inferential" and "noninferential" evidence of God's existence (sometimes referred to as propositional and nonpropositional evidence), John Bishop captures the distinction well when he writes:

> A proposition's truth is inferentially evident when its truth is correctly inferable ... from other propositions whose truth is accepted; a proposition's truth is non-inferentially (basically) evident when its truth is acceptable . . . without being derived by inference from other evidentially established truths.[10]

Consider, on the one hand, the classical arguments for God's existence—the ontological, cosmological, and teleological arguments. Each of these arguments consists of an attempt to establish the truth of the proposition "God exists" by inferring it from other propositions that are accepted as true. Accordingly, each of these arguments involves inferential evidence. Consider, on the other hand, the argument from religious experience. This argument consists of an attempt to establish the truth of the proposition "God exists" not by inferring it from other evidentially established truths, but on the basis of direct perception or awareness of God. Accordingly, the argument from religious experience involves noninferential evidence.

Though public and private evidence, on the one hand, and inferential and noninferential evidence, on the other, are conceptually distinct, they nevertheless overlap in certain ways. One way in which they overlap is that inferential and noninferential evidence can be both public and private in nature. Each of the classical arguments for God's existence, for example, involves inferential, public evidence. A veridical appearance of God to a group of people is noninferential, public evidence. A suffering individual's plea to God that he (God) relieve his pain, immediately followed by the alleviation of said pain is inferential, private evidence. And, an individual-specific religious experience wherein God presents himself to the individual is noninferential, private evidence.

Having addressed the concept of evidence and, with it, the public/private and inferential/noninferential distinctions, let us turn to probabilifying evidence. Evidence comes in degrees of strength, of course, ranging from the very weak to the very strong. We acknowledge this, Nicholas Everitt submits, by our use of locutions of the following forms:

a. A proves B beyond all doubt.
b. A is overwhelming evidence for B.
c. A is very strong evidence for B.
d. A is strong evidence for B.
e. A makes B more likely than not.
f. A is good evidence of B.
g. A is fairly good evidence of B.
h. A makes B a real possibility.

[10] John Bishop (2007), *Believing by Faith: An Essay in the Epistemology and Ethics of Religious Belief.* Oxford: Clarendon Press, 23.

i. A suggests that B is possible.
j. A is some evidence of B.
k. A is weak evidence of B.
l. A marginally increases the likelihood that B is possible.[11]

For present purposes, by "probabilifying" evidence, I mean evidence captured by (a)–(e)—it is evidence that, minimally, makes the truth of a belief more likely than not and, maximally, proves the truth of a belief beyond all doubt. Clearly, evidence for the belief that God exists is not always probabilifying. An unexplained, seemingly supernatural event may be evidence of the existence of God, but it is not probabilifying evidence—it does not, in and of itself, render the belief that God exists more likely than not to be true, much less prove the belief that God exists beyond all doubt. Probabilifying evidence for the belief that God exists does just that—at a minimum, it renders the belief that God exists more likely than not to be true.

(One might reasonably wonder what *makes* probabilifying evidence probabilifying. This is a very important and very difficult question to answer. Fortunately (for my sake), this question need not be answered here, since I am critiquing each type of theistic philosopher on his or her own terms. And, for present purposes, it suffices to know that theistic inferentialists and theistic noninferentialists believe that there is probabilifying evidence of God's existence, and that theistic fideists do not.)

With regard to probabilifying evidence being "discoverable"—not simply in principle, but in practice—perhaps the best way to convey what I mean by this is to contrast it with some alternatives. First, one might believe that evidence of God's existence exists, but that it is in *principle* impossible to discover. J. L. Schellenberg refers to this as "undiscoverable evidence."[12] Undiscoverable evidence is evidence that we are incapable of recognizing "because it is in *principle* impossible for beings like us ever—in any time—to assimilate this information."[13] To motivate the idea of undiscoverable evidence, Schellenberg continues,

> Here we have to imagine that all the intellectual evolution we are capable of has taken place, and think about what might still lie outside our grasp when that has occurred. Would there be anything at all? The truth of an affirmative answer can surely not be ruled out. It is hard to believe that humans, being finite, will ever be capable of knowing everything there is to be known; no matter how far they develop, there must always remain the disturbing possibility of "that which cannot be understood." Accordingly, we must also take note of how there may be undiscoverable evidence with a bearing on beliefs of interest to us.[14]

An analogy may be useful here. Consider intelligent extraterrestrials who have intellectually evolved as much as they are capable of evolving but, nevertheless, lack the

---

[11] Everitt, *The Non-existence of God*, 13.
[12] J. L. Schellenberg (2007), *The Wisdom to Doubt: A Justification of Religious Skepticism*. Ithaca, NY: Cornell University Press, 24ff.
[13] Ibid., 18.
[14] Ibid., 24–5.

capacity to grasp the concept of perfection. For such extraterrestrials, evidence in the form of the concept of perfection is undiscoverable evidence.

Second, one might believe that evidence of God's existence exists, that the evidence is in principle possible to discover, but that it is in *practice* improbable, if not impossible, to discover. Evidence of this sort may fall into one of two categories—what Schellenberg refers to as "inaccessible evidence" and "undiscovered evidence."[15] Inaccessible evidence is "evidence one is capable of seeing, but it goes unrecognized because it is not part of one's own evidence: here unavoidable features of human intellectual life contingently prevent one from undertaking the investigation that would have led to an encounter with the evidence in question had one undertaken it."[16] Unlike with undiscoverable evidence, one is capable of recognizing inaccessible evidence; it is simply that one does not recognize it since, through no fault of one's own, it happens to fall outside one's range of apprehension. Consider, again, the aforementioned extraterrestrials. Suppose (contrary to the preceding example) that these extraterrestrials have intellectually evolved in such a way that they have the capacity to grasp the concept of perfection. Suppose also that, through no fault of their own, the concept of perfection falls outside their range of apprehension. For such extraterrestrials, evidence in the form of the concept of perfection is inaccessible evidence.

Undiscovered evidence, however, is "evidence we fail to see because we are not capable of seeing it in our time, in a manner deriving from limited development within what is possible in evolutionary terms (unevolved concepts or dispositions, primitive intellectual environment or resources, etc.)."[17] To use the example of the extraterrestrials once more, suppose they are intellectually evolving in such a way that they currently lack the capacity to grasp the concept of perfection, but their descendants will not only acquire that capacity, but also grasp the concept of perfection. For such extraterrestrials, evidence in the form of the concept of perfection is undiscovered evidence.

Theistic inferentialists and theistic noninferentialists, on the one hand, reject the view that all evidence of God's existence is undiscoverable—that all evidence of God's existence is, in principle, impossible to discover. They also reject the view that all evidence of God's existence is inaccessible or undiscovered—that all evidence of God's existence is in practice improbable, if not impossible, to discover. (They accept, however, that *some* evidence of God's existence may be inaccessible or undiscovered or undiscoverable.) Theistic fideists, on the other hand, hold that all evidence of God's existence is inaccessible or undiscovered or undiscoverable—that all evidence of God's existence is, in practice if not in principle, impossible to discover.

---

[15] Ibid., 21–4. Schellenberg also proposes the categories of "overlooked evidence" and "neglected evidence." It should be acknowledged that one could believe that evidence of God's existence exists, that the evidence is in principle possible to discover, but that it is in practice improbable, if not impossible, to discover due to overlooking or neglecting the evidence.

[16] Ibid., 18.

[17] Ibid., 18.

Theistic inferentialists, theistic noninferentialists, and theistic fideists

With the preceding concepts and distinctions in mind, let us take a closer look at each of the three types of theistic philosopher to be examined here. Perhaps the best way to conceptually motivate each of these types of theistic philosopher is by way of example. In the following, I will provide brief examples of each of them. Specifically, for each example of theistic philosopher to be considered below, I will present a condensed version of his argument for believing in God's existence. These arguments will also serve as touchstones for the rest of the book.

Theistic inferentialists

We begin with theistic inferentialists—philosophers who believe that (a) God exists, (b) there is inferential probabilifying evidence of God's existence, and (c) this evidence is discoverable not simply in principle, but in practice. Though the list of theistic inferentialists is quite long, we will consider just three here—William Paley, William Lane Craig, and Robin Collins.

Consider, first, William Paley and his version of the teleological argument. Paley observes that many natural parts of the universe (such as human eyes) resemble machines (such as telescopes) in that both human eyes and telescopes are what William Rowe calls "teleological systems"—systems of parts in which the parts are so arranged that, under proper conditions, they work together to serve certain purposes.[18] As Paley puts it,

> there is precisely the same proof that the eye was made for vision, as there is that the telescope was made for assisting it. They were made upon the same principles; both being adjusted to the laws by which the transmission and reflection of rays of light are regulated. I speak not of the origin of the laws themselves; but such laws being fixed, the construction, in both cases, is adapted to them . . . What could a mathematical instrument-maker have done more, to show his knowledge of his principle, his application of that knowledge, his suiting of his means to his end; I will not say to display the compass or excellence of his skill and art . . . but to testify counsel, choice, consideration, purpose?[19]

From this, Paley infers that it is likely that God exists. His argument may be summarized as follows:

P1: Machines (such as telescopes) are produced by intelligent design.
P2: Many natural parts of the universe (such as human eyes) resemble machines.

---

[18] Rowe, 57.
[19] William Paley (2009), "The Argument to Design," In Steven M. Cahn (ed.), *Exploring Philosophy of Religion: An Introductory Anthology.* New York, NY: Oxford University Press, 77.

C1: Probably, many natural parts of the universe are also produced by intelligent design.

P3: Probably, God is the designer of these many natural parts of the universe.

C2: Probably, God exists.[20]

Since Paley believes there is inferential probabilifying evidence of God's existence in the form of the teleological argument, he is thereby a theistic inferentialist.

Consider, next, William Lane Craig and his version of the Kalām cosmological argument. Craig argues that since everything that begins to exist has a cause, and since the universe began to exist, it is likely that God exists. That everything that begins to exist *does* have a cause strikes Craig as relatively uncontroversial. Indeed, it is "based on the intuition that something cannot come out of nothing. Hence, any argument for the principle is apt to be less obvious than the principle itself."[21] With this in mind, Craig continues,

> With regard to the universe, if originally there were absolutely nothing—no God, no space, no time—then how could the universe possibly come to exist? The truth of the principle *ex nihilo, nihil fit* (out of nothing, nothing comes) is so obvious that I think we are justified in forgoing an elaborate defense of the [claim "everything that begins to exist has a cause"].[22]

Craig's argument may be summarized as follows:

P1: Everything that begins to exist has a cause.

P2: The universe began to exist.

C1: The universe has a cause.

P3: Probably, God is the cause of the universe.

C2: Probably, God exists.[23]

Since Craig believes there is inferential probabilifying evidence of God's existence in the form of the Kalām cosmological argument, he is thereby a theistic inferentialist.

Finally, consider Robin Collins and his version of the teleological argument. Collins argues for the existence of God on the basis of the fine-tuning of the universe. In short, were the universe not finely tuned in the way that it is, life on earth would be impossible. And, that the universe is so finely tuned is not unlikely under theism, but is unlikely under atheism.[24] Regarding the claim that a finely tuned universe is not unlikely under theism, he argues, "Since God is an all good being, and it is good for

---

[20] This is a modified version of an argument found in Rowe, 55.

[21] William Lane Craig (2010), "The Kalām Cosmological Argument," In Michael Peterson, et al. *Philosophy of Religion: Selected Readings*, 4th edition. New York, NY: Oxford University Press, 203.

[22] Ibid., 203.

[23] This is a modified version of an argument found in William Lane Craig and J. P. Moreland (2008), "The Kalām Cosmological Argument," In Louis P. Pojman and Michael Rea (eds), *Philosophy of Religion: An Anthology*, 5th edition. Belmont, CA: Thomson Wadsworth, 36.

[24] Specifically, under the atheistic single-universe hypothesis, which states that there is only one universe and it is ultimately unexplainable.

intelligent, conscious beings to exist, it is not surprising or improbable that God would create a world that could support intelligent life."[25]

As for the claim that a finely tuned universe is unlikely under atheism, Collins defends it by way of analogy. He asks us to consider a mission to Mars wherein a domed structure is discovered. With a temperature of around 70 degrees, a humidity of 50 percent, an oxygen recycling system, an energy gathering system, etc., this domed structure is set up just right for life to exist. "What conclusion would we draw from finding this structure?" Collins asks. "Would we draw the conclusion that it just happened to form by chance? Certainly not."[26] After all, he asserts, that such a structure could be formed by chance is extremely unlikely. And so it is, Collins contends, with the finely tuned universe we find ourselves inhabiting. Collins' fine-tuning argument for God's existence may be summarized as follows:

P1: The universe is finely tuned.
P2: The existence of the fine-tuning is not improbable under theism.
P3: The existence of the fine-tuning is very improbable under atheism.
C: Probably, God exists.[27]

Since Collins believes there is inferential probabilifying evidence of God's existence in the form of the teleological argument, he is thereby a theistic inferentialist.

Theistic noninferentialists

Let us now consider examples of theistic noninferentialists—philosophers who believe that (a) God exists, (b) there is noninferential probabilifying evidence of God's existence, and (c) this evidence is discoverable not simply in principle, but in practice.

As indicated above, experiences can serve as direct, noninferential evidence of the existence of things. As such, religious experiences—such as experiences of God—can serve as noninferential probabilifying evidence of God's existence. Everitt effectively summarizes this view when he writes,

> Proponents of the view that religious experience can significantly raise the probability that God exists . . . often insist that the appeal to religious experience is not simply one more *argument* or *piece of reasoning* for the existence of God . . . Rather, they insist, it is not an *argument* at all . . . The point they are making is that experience gives a *direct* way of knowing about things, as distinct from the indirect, inferential way provided by having to reason our way to knowledge of them.[28]

---

[25] Robin Collins, "A Scientific Argument for the Existence of God," In *Philosophy of Religion: An Anthology*, 78.

[26] Ibid., 74.

[27] This is a modified version of an argument found in Collins, "A Scientific Argument for the Existence of God," 77.

[28] Everitt, *The Non-existence of God*, 150–1. It should be noted that some philosophers argue that religious experiences might be instances of *inferential*—rather than *noninferential*—evidence of God's existence. See Michael Martin (1990), *Atheism: A Philosophical Justification*. Philadelphia: Temple University Press, 156ff.

Each of the three theistic noninferentialists to be considered here—William Alston, Richard Swinburne, and Alvin Plantinga—appeals to experiences of one sort or another as noninferential evidence of God's existence.

William Alston argues there is noninferential probabilifying evidence of God's existence in the form of experiences of God. His argument involves comparing experiences of God to ordinary perception. Ordinary sensory perception—what Alston refers to as our "perceptual practice" (or, *PP*)—involves three elements—a perceiver, a perceived object, and an experience of the perceived object.[29] The perception of a typewriter, for example, involves a perceiver (the one perceiving the typewriter), a perceived object (the typewriter), and the experience of the perceived object (the awareness the perceiver has of the typewriter). And, barring reasons for thinking that the perception is hallucinatory or otherwise delusory (i.e., barring defeaters), the perception serves as noninferential probabilifying evidence of the typewriter's existence. As Alston writes,

> If I am justified, just by virtue of having the visual experiences I am now having, in taking what I am experiencing to be a typewriter situated directly in front of me, then the belief that there is a typewriter directly in front of me is directly justified by that experience.[30]

Similarly, experiences of God—of which Alston writes in terms of "Christian epistemic practice" (or, *CP*)—involve a perceiver (the one perceiving God), a perceived object (God), and the experience of the perceived object (the awareness the perceiver has of God). And, barring defeaters, the perception serves as noninferential probabilifying evidence of God's existence. As Alston puts it,

> When . . . someone takes himself to be experiencing the presence of God, he thinks that his experience justifies him in supposing that God is what he is experiencing. Thus, he supposes himself to be directly justified by his experience in believing God to be present to him.[31]

He concludes that "*CP* has basically the same epistemic status as *PP* and that no one who subscribes to the latter is in any position to cavil at the former."[32] Alston's argument may be summarized as follows:

P1: It epistemically seems to subjects of experiences of God that God is present.
P2: If it epistemically seems to subjects of experiences of God that God is present, then probably God is present, unless there are defeaters.
C: Probably God is present, unless there are defeaters.[33]

---

[29] See Michael Peterson, et al. (2009), *Reason & Religious Belief: An Introduction to the Philosophy of Religion*, 4th edition. New York, NY: Oxford University Press, 33.
[30] William Alston, "Religious Experience and Religious Belief," In *Philosophy of Religion: An Anthology*, 137.
[31] Ibid., 137.
[32] Ibid., 142.
[33] This is a modified version of an argument found in Richard M. Gale (2007), *On the Philosophy of Religion*. Belmont, CA: Thomson Wadsworth, 58-9.

Since Alston believes there is noninferential probabilifying evidence of God's existence in the form of experiences of God, he is thereby a theistic noninferentialist.

Like Alston, Richard Swinburne argues that there is noninferential probabilifying evidence of God's existence in the form of experiences of God. Swinburne begins with the claim that "An apparent experience . . . is a real experience . . . if it is caused by that of which it purports to be an experience."[34] With this in mind, he continues:

> Now it is evident that, rightly or wrongly, it has seemed (in the epistemic sense) to millions and millions of humans that at any rate once or twice in their lives they have been aware of God and his guidance . . . They may be mistaken, but that is the way it has seemed to them. Now it is a basic principle of rationality, which I call the principle of credulity, that we ought to believe that things are as they seem to be (in the epistemic sense) unless and until we have evidence that we are mistaken . . . Someone who seems to have an experience of God should believe that he does, unless evidence can be produced that he is mistaken.[35]

Swinburne's argument may be summarized as follows:

P1: We ought to believe that things are as they seem to be unless and until we have evidence that we are mistaken.
P2: It seems to some people that they are having an experience of God.
C: These people ought to believe that things are as they seem to be—that they *are* having an experience of God—unless and until they have evidence that they are mistaken.

Since Swinburne believes there is noninferential probabilifying evidence of God's existence in the form of experiences of God, he is thereby a theistic noninferentialist.

Finally, consider Alvin Plantinga. According to Plantinga, the belief that God exists is properly basic. A properly basic belief is a belief one is justified in holding whose justification is not a function of inferential reasoning. Examples of properly basic beliefs include the beliefs that $2 + 2 = 4$, that the external world exists, that other people are not actually robots, that one is being appeared to in a particular way, and that one's memories tend to be reliable. According to Plantinga, each of these beliefs is *basic* in that none is inferred from other beliefs. And each is *properly* basic in that each is a belief one is justified in holding whose justification is not a function of inferential reasoning.

And so it is, Plantinga argues, with respect to the belief that God exists. The belief that God exists is basic in that it is not (at least, need not be) inferred from other beliefs. And, it is properly basic in that it is a belief one is justified in holding whose justification is not a function of inferential reasoning. According to Plantinga, each one of us has been created by God in such a way that we are disposed to believe that God exists, and this disposition may be triggered by a wide variety of circumstances,

[34] Richard Swinburne (1996), *Is There A God?* New York, NY: Oxford University Press, 131.
[35] Swinburne, *Is There A God?*, 131–3.

such as upon beholding the stars above or the beauty of a flower. And, when a person's disposition to believe that God exists is triggered by such circumstances,

> [i]t isn't that such a person is justified or rational in so believing by virtue of having an implicit argument—some version of the teleological argument, say. No; he doesn't need any argument for justification or rationality. His belief need not be based on any other propositions at all; under these conditions he is perfectly rational in accepting belief in God in the utter absence of any argument, deductive or inductive. Indeed, a person in these conditions . . . *knows* that God exists, has knowledge of God's existence, apart from any argument at all.[36]

Before summarizing Plantinga's argument, it should be noted here that some philosophers have mistakenly taken these comments to mean that, as properly basic, belief in God's existence is not based on evidence. As one philosopher writes, "With respect to belief in God, Plantinga contends that one does not need arguments *or evidence* for that belief to be rational."[37] But this is a misreading of Plantinga. What Plantinga argues is that, as properly basic, belief in God's existence is not based on *inferential* evidence; he does *not* argue that properly basic belief in God's existence is not based on any evidence whatsoever. As he states in another work:

> In my opening statement, I argued that the proper position here, for the theist, is that belief in God *is* noninferentially justified—i.e., that there is *powerful non-propositional evidence* or grounds for the existence of God. The sensible thing for a theist to think is that there is what Aquinas calls a natural knowledge of God, or something like what John Calvin called a "*Sensus divinitatis*." This would be a cognitive faculty or process, built into us by God, that delivers beliefs about God under a wide variety of circumstances . . . *So of course I believe that there is positive evidence—non-propositional evidence—for the existence of God*, just as there is for external objects, and the past.[38]

Plantinga holds, then, that properly basic belief in God's existence serves as noninferential evidence of God's existence. His argument may be summarized as follows:

P1: If the belief that God exists is properly basic, then there is noninferential probabilifying evidence of God's existence.

---

[36] Alvin Plantinga, "Belief Without Argument," In *Exploring Philosophy of Religion: An Introductory Anthology*, 220.

[37] Kelly James Clark (1997), "Introduction," In *Philosophers Who Believe: The Spiritual Journeys of 11 Leading Thinkers*. Downers Grove, IL: Intervarsity Press, 14, emphasis mine. Ironically, Plantinga makes this rather clear in the very volume in which these comments are made. In his defense of belief in God being properly basic, Plantinga writes, "my main aim was to argue that it is perfectly rational to take belief in God as basic—to accept it, that is, without accepting it on the basis of argument or *evidence from other propositions one believes*" (Alvin Plantinga, "A Christian Life Partly Lived," In *Philosophers Who Believe*, 74, emphasis mine).

[38] Alvin Plantinga and Michael Tooley (2008), *Knowledge of God*. Malden, MA: Blackwell, 164–5, emphasis mine. As Richard Gale writes, despite his critique of the need for inferential evidence of God existence, "Plantinga is no fideist" (Gale, 118).

P2: The belief that God exists is properly basic.

C: There is noninferential probabilifying evidence of God's existence.[39]

Since Plantinga believes there is noninferential probabilifying evidence of God's existence in the form of properly basic belief in his existence, he is thereby a theistic noninferentialist.

(As stated above, one can be at once a theistic inferentialist and a theistic noninferentialist. Swinburne and Plantinga are examples of such philosophers. Swinburne thinks that there is inferential probabilifying evidence of God's existence in the form of the teleological and cosmological arguments, among others.[40] And Plantinga thinks that "there are a large number (at least a couple of dozen) good arguments for the existence of God."[41])

Theistic fideists

Finally, let us consider examples of theistic fideists, philosophers who believe that (a) God exists, (b) there is no discoverable probabilifying evidence of God's existence, but (c) it is acceptable—morally, if not otherwise—to have faith that God exists. We'll consider three here—Blaise Pascal, Søren Kierkegaard, and John Bishop.

Pascal argues that, since God has neither parts nor limits, he is infinitely incomprehensible to us. As a result, reason cannot decide whether or not God exists. With this in mind, he writes,

> Who will then blame the Christians for being unable to provide a rational basis for their belief, they who profess a religion for which they cannot provide a rational basis? They declare that it is a folly . . . in laying it before the world: and then you complain that they do not prove it! If they did prove it, they would not be keeping their word.[42]

Nevertheless, Pascal contends, we are forced to wager one way or the other on God's existence—refusing to wager is not an option since it amounts to wagering that God does not exist. Given this, we should wager that God exists, since wagering that God exists is better than wagering that he does not exist. For, by wagering that God exists, we have everything to gain and nothing to lose; while by wagering that God does not exist, we have nothing to gain and everything to lose. As he puts it,

> Let us weigh up the gain and the loss by calling heads that God exists. Let us assess the two cases: if you win, you win everything; if you lose, you lose nothing. Wager that he exists then, without hesitating![43]

---

[39] This is a modified version of an argument found in Plantinga, "Belief Without Argument," 218–27.

[40] See Swinburne's *The Existence of God* and *Is There A God?*.

[41] Alvin Plantinga (2000), *Warranted Christian Belief*. Oxford: Oxford University Press, 170. One such argument is his version of the ontological argument (see Alvin Plantinga (1991), *God, Freedom, and Evil*. Grand Rapids, MI: Wm. B. Eerdmans Publishing, Co., 85ff).

[42] Blaise Pascal, "The Wager," in *Exploring Philosophy of Religion*, 191.

[43] Ibid., 192.

And, if we should wager that God exists, then it is morally acceptable to believe that God exists independent of probabilifying evidence—at least, such is what is implied. After all, if believing that God exists independent of probabilifying evidence is (seriously) immoral, then it may be that, all things considered, we should *not* believe that God exists independent of probabilifying evidence. Pascal's argument for the moral acceptability of having faith that God exists may be summarized as follows:

P1: There is no discoverable probabilifying evidence of God's existence.
C1: If we are to believe that God exists, we must do so independent of probabilifying evidence—that is, we must have faith that God exists.
P2: We *are* to believe that God exists, since we have everything to gain and nothing to lose.
C2: We must have faith that God exists.
P3: If we must have faith that God exists, then having faith that God exists is morally acceptable.
C3: Having faith that God exists is morally acceptable.

Since Pascal believes there is no discoverable probabilifying evidence of God's existence, but that, nevertheless, it is morally acceptable to have faith that God exists, he is thereby a theistic fideist.

As for Kierkegaard, he claims that "every moment is wasted in which [one] does not have God."[44] However, Kierkegaard also argues that we do not have probabilifying evidence of God's existence because it is simply not available and, perhaps more importantly, because if it were available, we could not have that which is essential when it comes to believing that God exists—faith. As he puts it,

Without risk there is no faith. Faith is precisely the contradiction between the infinite passion of the individual's inwardness and the objective uncertainty. If I am capable of grasping God objectively, I do not believe, but precisely because I cannot do this I must believe. If I wish to preserve myself in faith I must constantly be intent upon holding fast the objective uncertainty, so as to remain out upon the deep, over seventy thousand fathoms of water, still preserving my faith.[45]

According to Kierkegaard, then, if we must "have" God—believe that he exists, among other things—but cannot have him on the basis of probabilifying evidence, it is morally acceptable to have him independent of probabilifying evidence (at least, as with Pascal's wager, such is implied). Kierkegaard's argument for the moral acceptability of having faith that God exists may be summarized as follows:

P1: There is no discoverable probabilifying evidence of God's existence.
C1: If we are to believe that God exists, we must do so independent of probabilifying evidence—that is, we must have faith that God exists.

[44] Søren Kierkegaard (1941), *Concluding Unscientific Postscript*, trans. David E. Swenson and Walter Lowrie. Princeton, NJ: Princeton University Press, 178–9.
[45] Ibid., 182.

P2: We *are* to believe that God exists, since every moment is wasted in which we do not have God.

C2: We must have faith that God exists.

P3: If we must have faith that God exists, then having faith that God exists is morally acceptable.

C3: Having faith that God exists is morally acceptable.

Since Kierkegaard believes there is no discoverable probabilifying evidence of God's existence but that, nevertheless, it is morally acceptable to have faith that God exists, he is thereby a theistic fideist.

Finally, consider John Bishop. Bishop offers a William James-inspired defense of what he refers to as "supra-evidential fideism."[46] Bishop embraces what he calls the "thesis of evidential ambiguity," which accepts that "the question of God's existence is left open—perhaps even necessarily, because our overall evidence is equally viably interpreted either from a theistic or an atheistic perspective."[47] Given the thesis of evidential ambiguity, the question arises whether it is morally permissible to have faith that God exists. Bishop believes that it can be, based on what he calls the "J+" thesis (read as *Jamesian-plus* thesis):

(J+) Where *p* is a faith-proposition of the kind exemplified by the propositions taken to be true in the context of theistic faith, it is morally permissible for people to take *p* to be true with full weight in their practical reasoning while correctly judging that it is not the case that *p*'s truth is adequately supported by their total available evidence, if and only if:

    a. the question whether *p* presents itself to them as a genuine option; and

    b. the question whether *p* is essentially evidentially undecidable; and

    c. their nonevidential motivation for taking *p* to be true is of a morally acceptable type; and

    d. *p*'s being true conforms with correct morality.[48]

With the J+ thesis in mind, Bishop's argument for the moral permissibility of having faith that God exists may be summarized as follows:

P1: There is no discoverable probabilifying evidence of God's existence.

C1: If we are to believe that God exists, we must do so independent of probabilifying evidence—that is, we must have faith that God exists.

P2: Having faith that God exists is morally acceptable so long as doing so accords with the J+ thesis.

---

[46] Bishop, 25.

[47] Ibid., 1.

[48] Ibid., 165. A "genuine option" is a decision that is living, forced, and momentous. A "living" option is one in which the two competing hypotheses are real possibilities for the person deciding between them. A "forced" option is one in which the two competing hypotheses collectively constitute all the available possibilities—no third hypothesis is possible. And a "momentous" option is one which is unique, significant, and irreversible.

P3: In some cases, having faith that God exists accords with the J + thesis.

C2: In such cases, having faith that God exists is morally acceptable.

Since Bishop believes there is no discoverable probabilifying evidence of God's existence, but that, nevertheless, it is morally acceptable to have faith that God exists, he is thereby a theistic fideist.

Problems for theistic philosophers

Having presented in more detail each of the three types of theistic philosopher to be examined here, I am now in a position to introduce the problems they face, each of which will be discussed more thoroughly in the chapters to come.

The word "problem" has at least two different senses. One sense of "problem" is "a question to be considered, solved, or answered," while another is "a misgiving, objection, or complaint."[49] The problems for theistic philosophers to be discussed in the subsequent chapters are initially understood as problems in the first sense— as questions to be considered. Upon critical reflection, however, they come to be understood as problems in the second sense—as objections.

Let us begin with the problem theistic inferentialists face. Theistic inferentialists have skeptical counterparts, of course—nontheistic philosophers. The very existence of nontheistic philosophers makes it clear that theistic inferentialists have failed to make the inferential evidential case for theism to them. And *that* they have failed to do so is a problem, one that will be referred to as the "problem of the theistic inferentialists." The problem is this—if there is discoverable inferential probabilifying evidence of God's existence, why have theistic inferentialists failed to make the inferential evidential case for theism to nontheistic philosophers? (Miserably, I might add, if the survey is any indication.) There are a number of possible solutions to this. But, as I argue in Chapter 2, of the most plausible possible solutions, each is either inadequate or incompatible with theistic inferentialists' defining beliefs. Thus, the problem *of* the theistic inferentialists is a problem *for* theistic inferentialists.

Theistic noninferentialists face a problem that is similar to, but distinct from, the problem theistic inferentialists face—one that will be referred to as the "problem of the hiddenness of God." (Though I raise the problem of the hiddenness of God here with respect to noninferential evidence, it can be and has been raised with respect to inferential evidence as well.)[50] The problem is this—if there is discoverable noninferential probabilifying evidence of God's existence, why is this evidence so scarcely apprehended, if it is apprehended at all? It is as if God is hiding from most of

---

[49] http://www.thefreedictionary.com/problem.

[50] See J. L. Schellenberg (1993), *Divine Hiddenness and Human Reason.* Ithaca, NY: Cornell University Press.

us, if he even exists. There are a number of possible solutions to this problem, one of the most popular being that God's hiddenness is necessary if we are to have morally significant freedom and, with it, the ability to develop morally significant characters. In Chapter 3, I address this solution, arguing that it not only fails to adequately solve the problem of the hiddenness of God, it gives us reason to believe that God does not exist.

The problem theistic fideists face, one that will be referred to as the "problem of faith," is as follows—if there is no discoverable probabilifying evidence of God's existence, why think that it is morally acceptable to have faith that he exists? After all, that there is no discoverable probabilifying evidence of God's existence does not immediately *entail* that having faith that God exists is morally acceptable. Moreover, having faith that a belief is true may result in endangering, harming, and/or violating the rights of others. In this vein, I argue in Chapter 4 that there is at least one condition under which it is *prima facie* wrong to have faith that God exists—when one's belief that God exists will affect others and one has not attempted to believe that God exists on the basis of sufficient evidence.

Each type of theistic philosopher faces a particular problem, then, or so I shall argue. I shall also argue that all three types of theistic philosopher share two problems, what will be referred to as the "problem of skeptical theism" and the "problem of divine omniscience." Let us consider each of these problems in turn.

All three types of theistic philosopher assume that we can know what God would do (either in particular cases or in general, directly or indirectly). Theistic inferentialists and theistic noninferentialists, for example, assume we can know that God would allow for there to be discoverable inferential and noninferential probabilifying evidence of his existence (respectively). Theistic fideists, on the other hand, assume that we can know that God would *not* allow for there to be discoverable probabilifying evidence of his existence, that God would be pleased with our wagering on his existence (Pascal), that God would allow us to "have" him (Kierkegaard), and so on. Yet, not all theistic philosophers assume that we can know what God would do. Certain theistic philosophers, to be referred to here as "skeptical theistic philosophers," doubt that we can know what God would do, at least in some cases. So, a fundamental question arises—*can* we know what God would do? This will be referred to as the "problem of skeptical theism." And, in Chapter 5, I argue that, of the possible answers to this question, each produces a problem for all three types of theistic philosopher.

A second problem that all three types of theistic philosopher share is the belief that God—as essentially omniscient, omnipotent, and perfectly good—is a logically possible being. Many philosophers have attempted to demonstrate that this is false, usually by way of arguing that it is logically impossible for something to be essentially omniscient and/or essentially omnipotent and/or essentially perfectly good. In Chapter 6, I follow this strategy, arguing that it is logically impossible for God to be essentially omniscient. This will be referred to as the "problem of divine omniscience."

Conclusion

The battle over what I have suggested is a philosophical version of the Alamo—theism—has been and continues to be fought with ammunition both evidential and nonevidential in nature. The defenders of theism may be divided into three categories—theistic inferentialists, theistic noninferentialists, and theistic fideists. Each of these theistic philosophers faces a problem unique to his or her type, and they all share two problems. And, though these problems might not be entirely insurmountable, they give us additional reason to think that—like the defenders of the Alamo before them—theistic philosophers may be in the last throes of their defense.

2

A Problem for Theistic Inferentialists

Introduction

Most theistic philosophers are theistic inferentialists. Again, theistic inferentialists are philosophers who believe that (a) God exists, (b) there is inferential probabilifying evidence of God's existence, and (c) this evidence is discoverable not simply in principle, but in practice. Augustine of Hippo, Anselm of Canterbury, Thomas Aquinas, William Paley, Richard Swinburne, Alvin Plantinga, Robin Collins, William Lane Craig—each of these theistic philosophers is a theistic inferentialist, and they collectively comprise only a small fraction of the theistic philosophers who are theistic inferentialists.

Theistic inferentialists have skeptical counterparts, of course—nontheistic philosophers. The very existence of these epistemic peers makes it clear that theistic inferentialists have failed to make the inferential evidential case for theism to them.[1] And that they have failed to do so is a problem, or so I shall argue. I refer to this as the "problem of the theistic inferentialists." Specifically, I shall argue that the fact that theistic inferentialists have failed to make the inferential evidential case to nontheistic philosophers raises a problem—a question that needs to be answered. I shall then argue that—of the most plausible possible solutions to this problem—each is either inadequate or incompatible with theistic inferentialists' defining beliefs. Thus, I conclude that the problem *of* the theistic inferentialists— the question of why theistic inferentialists have failed to make their case to nontheistic philosophers—is a problem *for* theistic inferentialists—an objection to their defining beliefs.

To set the stage for a more detailed discussion of the problem of the theistic inferentialists, let us start with an analogy—that of the world-class archeologists and the undiscovered goblet.

---

[1] Regarding epistemic peers, Richard Feldman writes, "Let's say that people are *epistemic peers* when they are roughly equal with respect to intelligence, reasoning powers, background information, and so on" (Richard Feldman (2007), "Reasonable Religious Disagreement," In Louise M. Antony (ed.), *Philosophers without Gods: Meditations on Atheism and the Secular Life*. Oxford: Oxford University Press, 201). For more on this concept, see Graham Oppy, "Disagreement," *International Journal for Philosophy of Religion* 68: 187ff.

The case of the world-class archeologists
and the undiscovered goblet

Suppose there are thousands of world-class archeologists who believe that:

a. an ancient, long-discussed, but yet-to-be-discovered goblet exists,
b. there is inferential probabilifying evidence of the goblet's existence, and
c. this evidence is discoverable not simply in principle, but in practice.

These world-class archeologists are ideally suited to discover the inferential probabilifying evidence (hereafter, simply "evidence") of the goblet's existence, if there is any. For, first, as world-class archeologists, they are educationally, intellectually, and experientially suited to discover evidence of the goblet's existence, if there is any. Moreover, as a result of believing (a)–(c), they not only actively look for but expect to find evidence of the goblet's existence and thus, are dispositionally suited to discover evidence of the goblet's existence. Given their level of education, intelligence, experience as well as the nature of their disposition, if anyone is suited to discover evidence of the goblet's existence, it is these world-class archeologists.

Suppose, moreover, that these world-class archeologists have an even greater number of colleagues—with comparable levels of education, intelligence, and experience—who do not believe that the goblet exists and, consequently, are not actively looking for and expecting to find evidence of the goblet's existence. For the sake of identification, let us refer to the archeologists actively looking for and expecting to find evidence of the goblet's existence as the "believers" and those who are not as the "skeptics." The degree of doubt among the skeptics varies from one archeologist to another, but they all agree that the believers have yet to make the case that, more likely than not, the goblet exists.

Looking in from the outside, one may wonder why the believers have failed to make their case to the skeptics. After all, these believers are exceptionally qualified individuals and, along with their predecessors, have been actively looking for and expecting to find evidence of the goblet's existence for thousands of years now. That they have not silenced their skeptical counterparts with evidence of the goblet's existence gives rise to the question—why not? There are a number of possible solutions to this problem, including:

1. The believers have discovered evidence of the goblet's existence and adequately articulated this to the skeptics, but the skeptics have not noticed due to their (the skeptics') intellectual inferiority.
2. The believers have discovered evidence of the goblet's existence and adequately articulated this to the skeptics, but the skeptics have not noticed due to their dispositional inferiority.
3. The believers have discovered evidence of the goblet's existence, but they have been unable to adequately articulate this evidence to the skeptics.
4. The believers have not discovered evidence of the goblet's existence, but this is not a problem (an objection), since it does not follow from this that they won't.

5. The believers have not discovered evidence of the goblet's existence, but this is not a problem (an objection) since the skeptics have not discovered evidence of the nonexistence of the goblet and, in turn, silenced their believing counterparts with it.
6. The believers have failed to make their case to their skeptical counterparts, but this is not surprising and, in turn, is not a problem (an objection), since such is the nature of archeological disagreement.
7. One or more of the believers' defining beliefs—(a)-(c)—is false.
8. One or more of the believers' defining beliefs is cognitively meaningless.

These are among the most plausible possible solutions to the problem of the believers. Some of them may work together, of course. For example, perhaps (1) and (2) together adequately explain why the believers have failed to make their case to their skeptical counterparts. For present purposes, there is no need to analyze and evaluate these solutions, as the preceding is simply an attempt to illustrate and motivate the problem that is the focus of this chapter. Let us turn to it now.

The problem of the theistic inferentialists

Theistic inferentialists are ideally suited to discover inferential probabilifying evidence (again, simply "evidence") of God's existence, if there is any. For, first, as professional philosophers, they are educationally, intellectually, and experientially suited to discover evidence of God's existence, if there is any. Moreover, as a result of believing (a)-(c), theistic inferentialists not only actively look for, but expect to find evidence of God's existence, and thus, are dispositionally suited to discover evidence of God's existence. Given their level of education, intelligence, experience as well as the nature of their dispositions, if anyone is suited to discover evidence of God's existence, it is the theistic inferentialists.

Now, there are likely thousands if not tens of thousands of theistic inferentialists actively looking for and expecting to find evidence of God's existence. (When their predecessors are included, the number of theistic inferentialists is likely in the hundreds of thousands, if not millions.) Moreover, theistic inferentialists have an even greater number of colleagues—with a comparable level of education, intelligence, and experience—who do not believe that God exists and, consequently, do not expect to find evidence of God's existence, namely, the nontheistic philosophers. I say "an even greater number" since, again, only 15 percent of professional philosophers accept or lean toward theism, 73 percent accept or lean toward atheism, while the rest accept or lean toward "other" beliefs.[2] Since accepting or leaning toward atheism or "other" involves not accepting or leaning toward theism, an overwhelming 85 percent of these philosophy faculty members do not accept or lean toward theism. The degree of doubt

---

[2] http://philpapers.org/surveys/results.pl?affil=Target+faculty&areas0=0&areas_max=1&grain=coarse.

among nontheistic philosophers varies from one individual to another, but they all agree that theistic inferentialists have yet to make the case that, more likely than not, God exists.

Looking in from the outside, one wonders why theistic inferentialists of such education, intelligence, experience, and disposition have failed to make their case to their skeptical counterparts. I refer to this as the "problem of the theistic inferentialists." I refer to this as the problem of the *theistic inferentialists* because it is the theistic inferentialists who actively look for and expect to find evidence of God's existence. And, I refer to it as the *problem* of the theistic inferentialists since, again, problem can mean a question to be answered and, if there were such evidence, one wonders why theistic inferentialists have not silenced their skeptical counterparts with it by now. After all, these theistic inferentialists are exceptionally qualified individuals and, along with their predecessors, have been actively looking for and expecting to find evidence of God's existence for nearly two millennia now. That they have not silenced their skeptical counterparts with evidence of God's existence gives rise to the question—why not? There are, I submit, a number of possible solutions to this problem, which I will discuss shortly. But, before doing so, two caveats are in order.

First, given that I have chosen to refer to this problem as the problem of the theistic inferentialists, some might think that I am committing the *ad hominem* fallacy. But this is not the case since, fundamentally, what is at issue here is theistic inferentialists' defining beliefs—(a)–(c)—not the theistic inferentialists *themselves*. To be sure, the problem of the theistic inferentialists involves claims about theistic inferentialists themselves. But this is because theistic inferentialists are the most suited collectors and presenters of evidence of God's existence, if there is any—just as, in the case of the undiscovered goblet, the believers are the most suited collectors and presenters of evidence of the goblet's existence, if there is any. As such, claims about theistic inferentialists themselves—specifically, claims about their failure to make their case to their skeptical counterparts—are relevant and thereby nonfallacious.[3] In short, if (a)–(c) are true, as theistic inferentialists believe, and if theistic inferentialists are the most suited individuals to demonstrate this, then the fact that they have not done so—a claim about theistic inferentialists themselves—is relevant to determining whether (a)–(c) are indeed true.

Second, some might argue that the problem of the theistic inferentialists is question-begging, believing it implies that theistic inferentialists have lacked and continue to lack inferential probabilifying evidence of God's existence. But this is not the case. The problem of the theistic inferentialists is simply this—if there is discoverable inferential probabilifying evidence of God's existence, as theistic inferentialists believe, why have theistic inferentialists failed to make the inferential evidential case for theism to their skeptical counterparts with it? As one can see, this question begs no questions with respect to God's existence or the existence of evidence thereof.

---

[3] Not all ad hominem arguments are fallacious. See Douglas Walton (2008), *Informal Logic: A Pragmatic Approach*. New York, NY: Cambridge University Press, 190ff.

Solutions to the problem of the theistic inferentialists

There are a number of possible solutions to the problem of the theistic inferentialists. But, of the most plausible possible solutions, each is either inadequate or incompatible with the theistic inferentialists' defining beliefs. Let us begin with the inadequate solutions.

Inadequate solutions

1. *Theistic inferentialists have discovered evidence of God's existence and adequately articulated this to nontheistic philosophers, but nontheistic philosophers have not noticed due to their (nontheistic philosophers') intellectual inferiority.*

This solution strikes me as rather unlikely. Whether nontheistic philosophers *are* intellectually inferior to their theistic counterparts is an empirical matter. And I am not aware of any empirical study of this having been conducted, let alone having established that they are. Accordingly, barring simply assuming a theology of one sort or another to be true (Calvinism, for example, with its tenet of total depravity), it seems unlikely that nontheistic philosophers en masse are intellectually inferior to theistic inferentialists, just as it seems unlikely that theistic inferentialists en masse are intellectually inferior to nontheistic philosophers. Moreover, if theistic inferentialists *were* to believe that nontheistic philosophers are intellectually inferior by simply assuming a theology to be true, nontheistic philosophers could likewise assume an *a*theology to be true, one that entails that theistic inferentialists are the ones who are intellectually inferior—an atheology that includes, say, Freud's view that religious belief is comparable to a childhood neurosis.[4] This, of course, would do nothing more than lead to an impasse.[5]

Empirical studies and (a)theologies aside, it is very difficult to believe that the skeptical counterparts to Aquinas, Paley, Collins, Craig, et al.—Hume, Nietzsche, Schellenberg, Everitt, et al.—are intellectually inferior to theistic inferentialists in such a way that they do not sufficiently comprehend the evidence theistic inferentialists have adequately articulated (*ex hypothesi*) in favor of God's existence. Indeed, some of these philosophers have collaborated with and debated each other without accusing the other of (seriously) misunderstanding his own view.[6] This is not to say that misunderstandings between theistic inferentialists and their skeptical counterparts do not occur, only that it is unlikely that a general intellectual inferiority on the part of nontheistic philosophers suffices to explain why theistic inferentialists have failed to make their case to their skeptical counterparts.

---

[4] See Sigmund Freud (1989), *The Future of an Illusion*, Standard Edition. New York, NY: W. W. Norton & Company.

[5] Alvin Plantinga acknowledges that this sort of impasse may arise between nontheistic and theistic philosophers. See Alvin Plantinga (1996), "Epistemic Probability and Evil," In Daniel Howard-Snyder (ed.), *The Evidential Argument from Evil*. Bloomington, IN: Indiana University Press, 90–1.

[6] See, for example, Alvin Plantinga and Michael Tooley (2008), *Knowledge of God*. Malden, MA: Blackwell.

2. *Theistic inferentialists have discovered evidence of God's existence and adequately articulated this to nontheistic philosophers, but nontheistic philosophers have not noticed this due to their dispositional inferiority.*

By nontheistic philosophers' "dispositional inferiority," I mean to say that they are somehow culpably ignorant of the evidence of God's existence, perhaps because they have willfully rejected it or because they have willfully refused to consider it. Paul Moser argues along these lines, writing,

> People whose receptive attitude is closed to God's program of all-inclusive renewal by grace may be blinded from the available evidence for the reality of God. The evidence may be readily available . . . We need, however, appropriate "ears to hear and eyes to see" the available evidence. We need a change of receptive attitude to apprehend the available evidence in the right way.[7]

Similarly, Alvin Plantinga writes,

> Original sin involves both intellect and will; it is both cognitive and affective. On the one hand, it carries with it a sort of *blindness*, a sort of imperceptiveness, dullness and stupidity . . . But sin is also and perhaps primarily an *affective* disorder or malfunction. Our affections are skewed, directed to the wrong objects; we love and hate the wrong things. Instead of seeking first the kingdom of God, I am inclined to seek my own personal glorification and aggrandizement, bending all my efforts toward making myself look good . . . Were it not for sin and its effects, God's presence and glory would be as obvious and uncontroversial to us all as the presence of other minds, physical objects and the past.[8]

But, as with the preceding solution, whether nontheistic philosophers have willfully rejected evidence of God's existence or refused to consider it is an empirical matter. And I am not aware of any empirical study of this having been conducted, let alone having established that nontheistic philosophers are so culpably ignorant. So, again, barring simply assuming a theology of one sort or another to be true and, in turn, believing that nontheistic philosophers are so culpably ignorant, it seems unlikely that nontheistic philosophers en masse have willfully rejected evidence of God's existence or refused to consider it, just as it seems unlikely that theistic inferentialists en masse have willfully rejected evidence of the nonexistence of God or refused to consider it. And, again, if theistic inferentialists were to believe that nontheistic philosophers are dispositionally inferior by simply assuming a theology to be true, nontheistic philosophers could likewise assume an atheology to be true, one that entails that theistic inferentialists are

---

[7] Paul K. Moser (2004), *"Divine Hiddenness Does Not Justify Atheism,"* In Michael L. Peterson and Raymond J. Vanarragon (eds), *Contemporary Debates in Philosophy of Religion*. Malden, MA: Blackwell Publishing, 47.

[8] Alvin Plantinga (2000), *Warranted Christian Belief.* Oxford: Oxford University Press, 207–8 and 214.

the ones who are dispositionally inferior. This, again, would do nothing more than lead to an impasse.

Empirical studies and theologies aside, there is little doubt that *some* nontheistic philosophers have willfully rejected evidence of God's existence or refused to consider it—after all, everyone succumbs to irrational or nonrational factors from time to time. But that some may have done so does not explain why theistic inferentialists have failed to make their case to those nontheistic philosophers who have *not* willfully rejected evidence of God's existence or refused to consider it. Of course, theistic inferentialists might think that *all* nontheistic philosophers have willfully rejected evidence of God's existence or refused to consider it. But, again, without first assuming a theology to be true, this seems rather unlikely.

Another reason to think that this solution is inadequate has to do with the fact that theistic inferentialists argue with nontheistic philosophers over more than just God's existence. They also argue over issues of ethics, epistemology, aesthetics, logic, politics, science, and more. Now, hardly anyone—including theistic inferentialists themselves— would hold that, when it comes to disagreements between theistic inferentialists and their skeptical counterparts on these issues, an adequate explanation of this is that nontheistic philosophers are dispositionally inferior to theistic inferentialists. Why, then, would one think that, when it comes to disagreement between theistic inferentialists and nontheistic philosophers on another issue—namely, evidence of God's existence—an adequate explanation of this is that nontheistic philosophers are dispositionally inferior to theistic inferentialists? Once again, without first assuming a theology to be true, such an explanation seems unlikely.[9]

3. *Theistic inferentialists have discovered evidence of God's existence and adequately articulated this to nontheistic philosophers, but nontheistic philosophers have not noticed this due to God's preventing them from noticing.*

Specifically, perhaps God blinds nontheistic philosophers to the evidence of his existence, just as God hardened the Pharaoh's heart, according to the Old Testament.[10] And, perhaps he does this because nontheistic philosophers do not believe or are not disposed to believe that he exists.

There are a number of problems with this solution, the first of which is that it appears to be ad hoc. To motivate this, consider, again, the case of the undiscovered

---

[9] I find Nicholas Everitt's perspective on this issue to be delightfully stated:

> When you go to the optician for glasses, you expect her to tell you that your sight is defective because the lens in one eye has become cloudy, or the eye muscle is too weak to tighten the lens properly and bring objects into focus, etc. If you visit the hospital to discover why your memory is playing up, you expect to be told that you suffer from a deficiency of some neuro-transmitter, or you have a tumour on the brain . . . In no serious investigation of the cause of a cognitive malfunction would any properly informed person say "You are red/green colour blind because you are sinful" or "You are poor at detecting the fallacy of affirming the consequent because you are sinful." (Nicholas Everitt, *The Non-existence of God* (London: Routledge, 2009), 189)

[10] Exodus 10: 20.

goblet. Suppose the believers explained their failure to make their case to the skeptics on the grounds that evidence of the goblet may be found only by those who already believe—or, at least, are disposed to believe—that the goblet exists. This may be true, but looking in from the outside, such an explanation appears ad hoc. Or, to use a more suitable analogy, suppose members of Raëlism—a religion that teaches that life on Earth was scientifically created by a species of intelligent extraterrestrials—explained their failure to make their case to non-Raëlians on the grounds that the extraterrestrials blind them to the evidence of their existence. The evidence, they maintain, may be found only by those who already believe or are disposed to believe that the extraterrestrials exist.[11] This may be true, but looking in from the outside, such an explanation appears ad hoc. And so it is with this solution to the problem of the theistic inferentialists—it is possible that evidence of God's existence may be found only by those who already believe or are disposed to believe that God exists, but such an explanation appears ad hoc.

Of course, to appear to be ad hoc is not one and the same as actually being ad hoc. And, if the explanation under consideration is not actually ad hoc and is plausible, then it is likely . . . *if* God exists.[12] But, regarding plausibility, this explanation is simply implausible, for it implies that evidence may now be divided into two further categories:

    i. evidence that can be discovered regardless of whether one believes or is disposed to believe in the existence of that of which it is evidence, and,

    ii. evidence that can be discovered only if one believes or is disposed to believe in the existence of that of which it is evidence.

Now, every debate of which I have been aware heretofore—philosophical or other—relies upon evidence of the former sort. But, if this explanation is acceptable, then we would have to grant that the debate on God's existence—and perhaps many other debates—rely upon evidence of the latter sort. But this strikes me as implausible. To see why, consider the following.

Suppose you do not believe that Platonic Forms—or other minds, or extraterrestrials, or unicorns, etc.—exist, as you have not discovered evidence of these things. If the explanation under consideration is acceptable, it might be that the evidence you have been looking for is not the right sort of evidence for these things. It might be that the right sort of evidence for these things is the evidence that can be discovered only if one believes or is disposed to believe in the existence of that of which it is evidence. This may be possible, but it is rather implausible—one's believing or being disposed to believe that Platonic Forms—or other minds, or extraterrestrials, or unicorns—exist seems to have no bearing whatsoever on whether evidence thereof exists or can be discovered. To be sure, believing or being disposed to believe in the existence of *evidence* bears upon whether evidence can or will be discovered; after all, if one does

[11] http://www.rael.org/home.
[12] Thanks to Paul Draper for pointing this out.

not think that evidence exists, then one will not attempt to look for it. But, believing or being disposed to believe in the existence *of that of which it is evidence* seemingly does not. Granted, the sort of evidence that can be discovered only if one believes or is disposed to believe in the existence of that of which it is evidence may apply to only one thing—God. But this brings us full circle, as such appears ad hoc.

Regarding this explanation being likely if God exists, this may be true, but it is unlikely to render the solution under consideration adequate. Theistic inferentialists might find it to be adequate, to be sure, but I am certain that nontheistic philosophers will not, as the likelihood is conditional upon the truth of something they reject—theism. If more than just theistic inferentialists are to be satisfied with this explanation, we need to get beyond the conditional "If God exists, then explanation (3) is likely" to an affirmation of the antecedent "God exists" from which we may deduce "Explanation (3) is likely." But, in the present context, an explanation for why theistic inferentialists have failed to make their case to nontheistic philosophers that depends upon the truth of the claim "God exists" will be compelling only for theistic inferentialists themselves.

Finally, if theistic inferentialists accept the explanation under consideration and really believe that God prevents their skeptical counterparts from discovering evidence of his existence, why do they continue to participate in what, by their own lights, must be nothing more than a farce, namely, arguing with nontheistic philosophers over the issue of God's existence? Perhaps it is because they believe God has commanded them to do so, or because they enjoy doing so, or because they make money by doing so, or what have you. But, given the explanation under consideration, it cannot be because they believe that a genuine dialogue regarding the truth of the matter could be had with nontheistic philosophers.

4. *Theistic inferentialists have discovered evidence of God's existence, but they have been unable to adequately articulate this evidence to their skeptical counterparts.*

More specifically, it may be that the evidence there is of God's existence is difficult not simply to find, but to understand and articulate. (As C. Stephen Layman writes, "having evidence and being able to articulate it are two different things.")[13] Indeed, the most recent versions of the classical arguments for God's existence lend support to this possibility. Each of these arguments includes concepts and/or demonstrations that even theistic inferentialists have trouble understanding and performing (respectively). For example, a recent version of the Kalām cosmological argument invokes the concept of metaphysical time (not to be confused with physical time); a recent version of the ontological argument relies upon the modal concepts of possible worlds and maximal greatness as well as the S5 axiom of modal logic; recent versions of the cosmological and the teleological arguments employ Bayes' Theorem; and a recent version of the teleological argument involves attempting to demonstrate the irreducible complexity

---

[13] C. Stephen Layman (1996), "Faith Has Its Reasons," In Thomas V. Morris (ed.), *God and the Philosophers: The Reconciliation of Faith and Reason.* New York, NY: Oxford University Press, 97.

of things such as the bacterial flagellum and the immune system.[14] Needless to say, even the best of minds may have trouble adequately understanding and articulating to others evidence that relies on such concepts and demonstrations. In some cases, this is because the concepts employed are inherently difficult to understand. In others, it is because the demonstrations and the understandings thereof require a robust understanding of a nonphilosophical discipline, such as molecular biology.

Now, it may indeed be that the evidence there is of God's existence is difficult not only to find, but to understand and articulate. But, there is something very troubling about this solution. Simply put, it is baffling that God would decide to provide evidence of his existence, but do so in such a bizarre and obscure way; so bizarre and obscure that, *ex hypothesi*, those who are most suited to understand and articulate the evidence to nontheistic philosophers (theistic inferentialists) nevertheless fail to do so. (I write "decide" deliberately, since I am assuming that God could have prevented us from having evidence of his existence and that he would not leave the matter of evidence of his existence to chance.)[15]

To motivate this point, let us consider in greater detail some of the most recent versions of the classical arguments for God's existence, beginning with the version of the teleological argument that invokes the alleged irreducible complexity of the bacterial flagellum. (If you are wondering what irreducible complexity and bacterial flagella are, you are proving my point.) Proponents of this argument would have us believe that God has provided evidence of his existence and has done so in the form of the irreducible complexity of the bacterial flagellum. But it is very difficult to understand why God would do this, let alone believe it. Of all the places where God could have provided evidence of his existence—particularly biological evidence—are we to believe that he decided to provide it in the bacterial flagellum, something the existence and nature of which was known by no one prior to the development of molecular biology and is known by relatively few people even after the development of molecular biology? Indeed, genuinely appreciating this evidence requires something most of us do not have—an adequate understanding of molecular biology. That God has provided evidence of his existence in such a bizarre and obscure way is very difficult to understand, let alone believe.

Or, consider the version of the Kalām cosmological argument that relies upon the concept of metaphysical time. William Lane Craig invokes the concept of metaphysical

---

[14] See, respectively, William Lane Craig (1992), "The Origin and Creation of the Universe: A Response to Adolf Grünbaum," *British Journal for the Philosophy of Science* 43: 239; Alvin Plantinga (1991), *God, Freedom, and Evil*. Grand Rapids, MI: Wm. B. Eerdmans Publishing, Co., 85ff; Richard Swinburne (2004), *The Existence of God*, 2nd edition. Oxford: Oxford University Press, Chapters 7 and 8; and Michael Behe (1998), *Darwin's Black Box: The Biochemical Challenge to Evolution*. New York, NY: Free Press.

[15] God could have prevented us from having evidence of his existence by not leaving any evidence of his existence behind or by blinding us to the evidence. Regarding a defense of the view that God would not leave this matter—indeed, any matter—to chance, see Paul Helm (2004), "God Does Not Take Risks," In Michael L. Peterson and Raymond J. Vanarragon (eds), *Contemporary Debates in Philosophy of Religion*. New York, NY: Blackwell Publishing, 218–28.

time in order to explain states of affairs *prior* to the creation of the physical universe and, with it, physical time. As he describes it,

> [S]uppose that God led up to creation by counting, "1, 2, 3, . . ., fiat lux!" In that case, the series of mental events alone is sufficient to establish a temporal succession prior to the commencement of physical time at t = 0. There would be a sort of metaphysical time based on the succession of contents of consciousness in God's mind prior to the inception of physical time.[16]

Even assuming there can be (to employ Craig's hedge) "a sort of" metaphysical time along these lines, Wes Morriston's observation about metaphysical time cannot be overstated—"the nature of metaphysical time and its relation to physical time are large and difficult questions."[17] Of all the ways God could have provided evidence of his existence, are we to believe that he decided to provide it in a way that requires understanding of the concept of metaphysical time as well as its relation to physical time, a concept and a relation that even those who invoke them struggle to understand? This, too, is very difficult to understand, let alone believe.

Or, consider the versions of the cosmological and teleological arguments that employ Bayes' Theorem. Just understanding Bayes' Theorem can be challenging—at least for those of us not well versed in probability and confirmation theory—let alone understanding whether the cosmological and teleological arguments that rely upon it are sound. The theorem may be represented as follows:

$$p(h/e\&k) = [p(e/h\&k) \times p(h/k)]/p(e/k)$$

where "p" stands for "probability," "e" stands for "evidence," "h" stands for "hypothesis," and "k" stands for "background knowledge." In addition to understanding the theorem, establishing e, h, and k, and then determining the probabilities of these things can be very challenging. Even theistic inferentialists recognize this. For example, with regard to establishing the probabilities, Del Ratzsch states, "A difficulty which arises . . . is that Bayes' Theorem can only go from probabilities to probabilities, meaning that one is required to *begin* with some probability assignments before one can use the Theorem or its derivatives. And where does one *get* those prior probabilities?"[18] Philosophers, it appears, cannot agree on an answer.[19] It strains the limits of understanding and

---

[16] Craig, "The Origin and the Creation of the Universe: A Response to Adolph Grünbaum," 239.

[17] Wes Morriston (2002), "A Critique of the Kalām Cosmological Argument," In Ray Martin and Christopher Bernard (eds), *God Matters: Readings in the Philosophy of Religion*. New York, NY: Longman Press, 100.

[18] http://plato.stanford.edu/entries/teleological-arguments/.

[19] http://plato.stanford.edu/entries/teleological-arguments/. I am reminded here of a statement made by Richard Gale regarding Swinburne's *The Existence of God*, "One of the valuable lessons to be learned from Richard Swinburne's *The Existence of God*, which makes . . . a Bayesian case for belief, is that the issues are exceedingly complex and need to be treated by those who are steeped in probability and confirmation theory, which eliminates me" (Richard Gale (1993), *On the Nature and Existence of God*. Cambridge: Cambridge University Press, 1).

belief that God would decide to provide evidence of his existence, but do so in such an obscure way.

Finally, and for good measure, consider the version of the ontological argument that relies upon the modal concepts of possible worlds and maximal greatness as well as the S5 axiom of modal logic.[20] Just understanding the argument is challenging for some of the most philosophically trained minds, and no doubt, virtually impenetrable for the philosophically untrained mind (see footnote 20). Moreover, it relies upon dubious concepts and logical axioms. Take, for example, the concept of maximal greatness. According to this version of the ontological argument, maximal greatness is possibly exemplified. Yet, as Michael Tooley has argued, an argument formally similar to this version of the ontological argument can be developed, which entails that a property incompatible with maximal greatness is possibly exemplified as well—maximal evil.[21] This indicates that neither of these properties is possibly exemplified.

As for logical axioms, this version of the ontological argument depends on the S5 axiom of modal logic. According to the S5 axiom, if something is possibly necessary, then it is necessary. That is to say, what is possibly necessary is necessary in at least one possible world; thus, it is necessary and thereby true in all possible worlds.[22] And, with the S5 and other modal axioms in mind, James Garson writes,

> One could engage in endless argument over the correctness or incorrectness of these and other iteration principles for □ [it is necessary that] and ◊ [it is possible that]. The controversy can be partly resolved by recognizing that the words "necessarily" and "possibly" have many different uses. So the acceptability of axioms for modal logic depends on which of these uses we have in mind.[23]

---

[20] The argument may be stated as follows:

> P1: There is a possible world in which maximal greatness is instantiated.
> P2: Necessarily, a being is maximally great only if it has maximal excellence in every world.
> P3: Necessarily, a being has maximal excellence in every world only if it has omniscience, omnipotence, and moral perfection in every world.
> C1: There is a possible world W such that if it had been actual, then there would have existed a being that was omnipotent, omniscient, and morally perfect who would have had these qualities in every possible world.
> C2: If W would have been actual, it would have been impossible that there be no such being—that is, the proposition "there is no omnipotent, omniscient, morally perfect being" would have been an impossible proposition.
> P4: If a proposition is impossible in at least one possible world, then it is impossible in every possible world.
> C3: Therefore, "there is no omnipotent, omniscient, morally perfect being" is impossible in the actual world.
> C4: Therefore, there actually exists a being that is omnipotent, omniscient, and morally perfect.

See Plantinga, *God, Freedom, and Evil*, 111–12.

[21] Michael Tooley (1981), "Plantinga's Defense of the Ontological Argument," *Mind* 90: 422–7.
[22] http://plato.stanford.edu/entries/logic-modal/.
[23] Ibid.

That God would decide to provide evidence of his existence, but do so in such a way that "endless" argument may result over just the system of logic to use—let alone the claims entered into that system—is very difficult to understand, let alone believe.[24]

To be sure, God may not want evidence of his existence to be too obvious for one reason or another, or God may not *care* one way or the other whether we find evidence of his existence. But, regarding the former, providing evidence in the form of arguments involving the irreducible complexity of the bacterial flagellum, Bayes' Theorem, the concepts of possible worlds and metaphysical time, etc., in order to ensure that the evidence is not too obvious strikes me as overly cautious, especially when considered in light of the explanation under consideration. For, given the explanation under consideration, the evidence is so difficult to understand and adequately articulate that even those best suited to do so have failed thus far.

As for the latter, it may be that God does not care one way or the other whether we find evidence of his existence. But if theistic inferentialists believe this to be the case, then troubling questions arise—what reason does God have for deciding to provide any evidence of his existence whatsoever? For deciding to allow some of us to discover this evidence? For deciding to provide said evidence in the form of arguments involving the irreducible complexity of the bacterial flagellum, Bayes' Theorem, the concepts of possible worlds and metaphysical time, and so on? I ask for reasons for doing these things deliberately since, again, I am assuming that God could have prevented us from having evidence of his existence and that he would not leave the matter of evidence of his existence to chance. Why would God—who, *ex hypothesi*, does not care one way or the other whether we find evidence of his existence—decide nevertheless to provide evidence of his existence and do so in such a bizarre and obscure way? What is God thinking? It is so puzzling a possibility that, upon searching for reasons with just the slightest plausibility, I draw a blank. To motivate this point, consider the following analogy.

Suppose a woman gives birth to a child and immediately gives the child up for adoption. Thereafter, the child has no contact with his birthmother and, as far as the child knows, his adopted mother *is* his birthmother. Suppose, further, that the birthmother does not care one way or the other whether her child discovers evidence of her existence. Even so, she decides not only to provide evidence of her existence that her child may discover, but to do so in a bizarre and obscure way. For example, she decides to write letters about her existence to her child using Egyptian hieroglyphs, something very few people on the planet can understand and translate. And, she decides to secretly plant these letters in the chimney of the child's house, buried in the cement that fastens the bricks together. If the birthmother does not care one way or the other whether her child discovers evidence of her existence, what reason does she have for deciding to provide any evidence of her existence whatsoever? And, what reason does she have for providing said evidence in the form of letters written in Egyptian

---

[24] Georges Rey seems to share something of my sentiment in this regard when he writes, ". . . why should there be no *normal* evidence of [God's] existence?" (Georges Rey, "Meta-Atheism: Religious Avowal as Self-Deception," in *Philosophers Without Gods*, 260, emphasis mine).

hieroglyphs secretly buried between bricks in the chimney? What is the birthmother thinking?

There are, of course, many disanalogies between the birthmother and God. For example, the birthmother can have bad reasons for doing what she does while God cannot, and the letters are, in many ways, easier to discover than irreducibly complex bacterial flagella or Bayes' Theorem's requisite prior probabilities. But, I trust that the analogy serves the purpose of motivating the question—if God does not care one way or the other whether we find evidence of his existence, what reason does he have for deciding to provide evidence of his existence nevertheless and to do so in such a bizarre, obscure way? Even if God was simply thinking that he wanted to create irreducibly complex things just for kicks, as it were, he could have prevented us from discovering them. But, *ex hypothesi*, he did not prevent us from discovering them. So, again, what reason does God have for deciding to provide evidence of his existence and to do so in such a bizarre, obscure way? What is God thinking? I am not suggesting that no plausible answer to this question is forthcoming. But I am suggesting that, unless a plausible answer to this question is offered, the explanation under consideration is very difficult to believe, particularly when combined with the hypothesis that God does not care one way or the other whether we find evidence of his existence.[25]

Finally, many theistic inferentialists—such as Swinburne, Craig, and Aquinas—are exceptionally skilled at articulating philosophical concepts, distinctions, positions, and arguments. Given this, it is hard to believe that, when it comes to evidence of God's existence—Swinburne, Craig, and Aquinas's bread and butter, as it were—they simply have not been able to adequately articulate it to their skeptical counterparts.

5. *Theistic inferentialists have not discovered evidence of God's existence, but this is not a problem (an objection), since it does not follow from this that they won't.*

One might motivate this explanation by way of an analogy. Consider, for example, Fermat's Last Theorem.[26] It took over 350 years for someone to prove the theorem and, in the meantime, there was debate over whether a proof could ever be provided. The debate over God's existence may currently be in a similar situation—though God's existence has not been shown to be more probable than not, it will be.

The two cases, however, are significantly disanalogous. In the case of Fermat's Last Theorem, mathematicians believed that there was only one line of evidence that could prove Fermat's Last Theorem—a mathematical proof. In the case of God's existence, however, theistic inferentialists have believed and continue to believe that there are numerous lines of evidence that could establish the likelihood of God's existence— the ontological argument, the cosmological argument, the teleological argument, the argument from religious experience, the argument from miracles, the argument

---

[25] It should be noted here that I do not think that appeals to mystery or skeptical theism make for plausible answers to this question. Regarding appeals to mystery, see Chapter 3; regarding appeals to skeptical theism, see Chapter 5.

[26] According to the theorem, the equation $a^n + b^n = c^n$ cannot succeed for any exponent greater than two.

from morality, the argument from justice, the argument from scripture, the argument from cumulative evidence, and many more.[27] In other words, many more lines of evidence have been and continue to be available to theistic inferentialists from which they and their skeptical counterparts might infer God's existence than was available to mathematicians from which they could infer the provability of Fermat's Last Theorem. Even so, theistic inferentialists have failed to make the case for theism to their skeptical counterparts. That fact, as well as the fact that theistic inferentialists have been arguing for theism for nearly two millennia—over five times as long as mathematicians attempted to prove Fermat's Last Theorem—renders the two cases significantly disanalogous.

Accordingly, if *ex hypothesi*, theistic inferentialists have not found evidence of God's existence, it is very hard to believe that this could be anything but a problem. After nearly two millennia, with hundreds of thousands, if not millions, of the most suited individuals giving a tremendous amount of serious and critical thought to this issue, it is really hard to believe that all that is needed is more time. After all, by their own lights, theistic inferentialists are searching for evidence of a god who decided to provide many lines of evidence of his existence—evidence that is discoverable not simply in principle, but in practice.[28]

Also, as with the reply to solution (4), it is baffling that God would decide to provide evidence of his existence, but do so in such a way that so much time, energy, diligence, intelligence, expertise, and more is needed to find it.

6. *Theistic inferentialists have not discovered evidence of God's existence, but this is not a problem (an objection) since nontheistic philosophers have not discovered evidence of the nonexistence of God and, in turn, silenced their theistic counterparts with it.*

There are a number of problems with this solution. First, in the vein of solutions (4) and (5), if theistic inferentialists have not found evidence of God's existence thus far,

---

[27] See Michael Martin (1990), *Atheism: A Philosophical Justification*. Philadelphia: Temple University Press. Alvin Plantinga lists two dozen more arguments for God's existence, including the argument from intentionality, the argument from collections, the argument from natural numbers, the argument from counterfactuals, the argument from physical constants, the argument from positive epistemic status, the argument from induction, the argument from reference, the argument from colors and flavors, the Mozart argument, and the argument from play and enjoyment. See Alvin Plantinga, "Two Dozen (or so) Theistic Arguments," http://www.calvin.edu/academic/philosophy/virtual_library/articles/plantinga_alvin/two_dozen_or_so_theistic_arguments.pdf.

[28] J. L. Schellenberg has recently argued that two millennia is probably not enough time to settle, which is the correct version of what he calls "ultimism"—the view that there is an ultimate reality in relation to which an ultimate good can be attained. But, as is evidenced by his disproofs of God's existence, he thinks that two millennia *is* enough time with regard to *one version* of ultimism, namely, theism. As he writes,

> . . . I want to do more here than simply trot out some new arguments for atheism. I want to show that these arguments are forceful and powerful, threatening to prove the truth of their conclusion—that many of the claims on which they depend will appear to us as strong candidates for the status of "clear case" when we rip the veil of tradition and convention from our eyes. If I am right about this, then my arguments justify not just doubt but disbelief with respect to theism (J. L. Schellenberg, *The Wisdom to Doubt: A Justification of Religious Skepticism* (Ithaca, NY: Cornell University Press, 2007), 192–3).

it is very hard to believe that this could be anything but a problem. After nearly two millennia, with hundreds of thousands if not millions of the most suited individuals giving a tremendous amount of serious and critical thought to this issue, it is really hard to believe that such evidence exists, but that theistic inferentialists have not found it.

Second, it is not at all clear that nontheistic philosophers have not discovered evidence of the nonexistence of God; certainly, many atheistic philosophers believe they have discovered such evidence. From positive arguments (such as the argument from evil and the argument from divine hiddenness) to negative arguments (critiques of positive arguments for the existence of God), evidence of the nonexistence of God has been presented by atheistic philosophers. Of course, such evidence may be defective in one way or another. But it would be a mistake simply to assume from the outset that nontheistic philosophers have not discovered evidence of the nonexistence of God.

Third, even if nontheistic philosophers have not discovered evidence of the nonexistence of God, theistic inferentialists and nontheistic philosophers are not such strict counterparts such that, if failure to discover evidence of God's existence is a problem for theistic inferentialists, then failure to discover evidence of God's nonexistence is a problem for nontheistic philosophers. There is a significant difference between failure to discover evidence of the existence of something, and failure to discover evidence of the nonexistence of something. All else being equal, when one carefully and rigorously searches for evidence of something, X, where it is reasonable to expect to find evidence of X, failure to discover evidence of the existence of X is evidence of the nonexistence of X. On the other hand, when one carefully and rigorously searches for evidence of the nonexistence of X where it is reasonable to expect to find evidence of the nonexistence of X, failure to discover evidence of the nonexistence of X is not evidence of the existence of X, all else being equal.[29]

Consider, for example, the case of the undiscovered goblet—the believers' failure to discover evidence of the existence of the goblet is evidence of the nonexistence of the goblet; while the skeptics' failure to discover evidence of the nonexistence of the goblet is not evidence of the existence of the goblet. Or, consider Raëlism— the Raëlians' failure to discover evidence of the existence of the extraterrestrials

---

[29] Graham Oppy agrees, stating, "That I have failed to find reasons of such-and-such kind may well be evidence for the claim—may well make it more likely—that there are no reasons of such-and-such kind . . . To strengthen the case for this claim, we can add that the investigation has been neither careless nor casual: many people have devoted extensive effort to the search for reasons of the kind in question" (Graham Oppy (2006), *Arguing About Gods*. New York, NY: Cambridge University Press, 295–6 and 296, footnote 39). According to Giovanni Mion, this is explained by the logical structure of the proposition under consideration. Consider the following two forms of argument:

i. In spite of our efforts to establish p, we have no proof (knowledge, evidence) that p exists. Therefore, $\sim p$.
ii. In spite of our efforts to establish $\sim p$, we have no proof (knowledge, evidence) that $\sim p$ does not exist. Therefore, p.

Mion argues that if the logical structure of p is an existential empirical proposition—as is the case with the proposition "There is evidence of God's existence"—then the reasoning of (i) is not fallacious, while the reasoning of (ii) is. See Giovanni Mion (2012), "God, Ignorance, and Existence," *International Journal for Philosophy of Religion* 72(2): 85–8.

is evidence of the nonexistence of the extraterrestrials; while the skeptics' failure to discover evidence of the nonexistence of the extraterrestrials is not evidence of the existence of the extraterrestrials. Likewise, the theistic inferentialists' failure to discover evidence of the existence of God—evidence they believe exists and is discoverable in practice—is evidence of the nonexistence of God; while the nontheistic philosophers' failure to discover evidence of the nonexistence of God is not evidence of the existence of God. Given this, it is simply not the case that, if failure to discover evidence of God's existence is a problem for theistic inferentialists, then failure to discover evidence of God's nonexistence is a problem for nontheistic philosophers.

Finally, even if failure to discover evidence of God's nonexistence were a problem for nontheistic philosophers, it would not follow that theistic inferentialists' failure to discover evidence of God's existence is not a problem. If anything, what would follow is that both theistic inferentialists and nontheistic philosophers face a problem. If this were the case, perhaps theistic inferentialists and nontheistic philosophers would be wise to take more seriously the attitude Hume's character Philo has toward these matters—"Could you even blame me if I had answered, at first, *that I did not know*, and was sensible that this subject lay vastly beyond the reach of my faculties?"[30]

7. *Theistic inferentialists have failed to make their case to their skeptical counterparts, but this is not surprising and, in turn, not a problem (an objection), since such is the nature of philosophical disagreement.*

Granted, when it comes to philosophical disagreement, it may not be surprising that theistic inferentialists have failed to make their case to nontheistic philosophers. As Gideon Rosen writes,

> It should be obvious that reasonable people can disagree, even when confronted with a single body of evidence. When a jury or a court is divided in a difficult case, the mere fact of disagreement does not mean that someone is being unreasonable. Paleontologists disagree about what killed the dinosaurs. And while it is possible that most of the parties to this dispute are irrational, this need not be the case. To the contrary, it would appear to be a fact of epistemic life that a careful review of the evidence does not guarantee consensus, even among thoughtful and otherwise rational investigators.[31]

Indeed, it is hard to think of many philosophical disagreements that, after much debate, have resulted in a consensus.

---

[30] David Hume (2009), "The Argument to Design and the Problem of Evil," In Steven M. Cahn (ed.), *Exploring Philosophy of Religion: An Introductory Anthology.* New York, NY: Oxford University Press, 83. For an excellent defense of such skepticism, see Schellenberg, *The Wisdom to Doubt.*

[31] Gideon Rosen (2001), "Nominalism, Naturalism, and Philosophical Relativism," *Philosophical Perspectives* 15: 71–2.

Even so, it does not follow from this that theistic inferentialists' failure to make their case to nontheistic philosophers is not a problem. And, if what I am arguing here is correct, then the fact that they have so failed is problematic indeed. For, as stated previously, when a question goes inadequately answered, the former sense of "problem" (a question) gives rise to the latter sense of "problem" (an objection). Presently, I am arguing that, regarding the most plausible possible solutions, each is either inadequate or incompatible with theistic inferentialists' defining beliefs; thus, that the problem of the theistic inferentialists in the first sense of "problem" gives rise to a problem in the second sense of "problem." That the lack of an adequate answer is unsurprising does nothing to alleviate this.

What's more, recall that, when it comes to this particular philosophical disagreement, the vast majority of philosophers do not side with theistic inferentialists. So, though it may not be surprising that theistic inferentialists have failed to make their case to nontheistic philosophers, that they have failed to do so in such dramatic fashion bespeaks a problem indeed.

Adequate solutions

Having covered a number of inadequate solutions, I would like to conclude with two adequate solutions. They are adequate in a way similar to the way J. L. Mackie's "adequate solutions" to the logical problem of evil are adequate—they solve the problem, but not in a way theistic inferentialists will find agreeable. They are, after all, incompatible with theistic inferentialists' defining beliefs.[32]

8. *One or more of theistic inferentialists' defining beliefs—(a)–(c)—is false.*

Theistic inferentialists will not find this solution to be very attractive, of course; they are, after all, theistic inferentialists. Even so, were one to deny that God exists, or that inferential probabilifying evidence of God's existence exists, or that said evidence is discoverable not simply in principle, but in practice, then one could adequately explain why theistic inferentialists have failed to silence their skeptical counterparts with evidence of God's existence.

9. *One or more of theistic inferentialists' defining beliefs is cognitively meaningless.*

Like the preceding solution, theistic inferentialists will not find this solution to be very attractive. Even so, were one to hold that the belief that God exists—or that inferential probabilifying evidence of God's existence exists, or that said evidence is discoverable not simply in principle, but in practice—is cognitively meaningless and thereby neither true nor false, then one could adequately explain why theistic inferentialists have failed to silence their skeptical counterparts with evidence of God's existence.

---

[32]   See J. L. Mackie, "Evil and Omnipotence," in *Philosophy of Religion: An Anthology*, 174.

Conclusion

I have argued here that the fact that theistic inferentialists have failed to make the inferential evidential case for theism to nontheistic philosophers raises a problem—a question to be answered. I have also argued that—of the most plausible possible solutions to this problem—each is either inadequate or incompatible with theistic inferentialists' defining beliefs. Thus, I conclude that the problem *of* the theistic inferentialists is a problem *for* theistic inferentialists.

3

A Problem for Theistic Noninferentialists

Introduction

In the previous chapter, I argued that a problem theistic inferentialists face is that they have failed to make the inferential evidential case for theism to their skeptical counterparts. One adequate solution to this problem was that one or more of theistic inferentialists' defining beliefs is false. And, one such belief was that there is inferential probabilifying evidence of God's existence. This brings us to theistic noninferentialists, philosophers who believe that (a) God exists, (b) there is *noninferential* probabilifying evidence of God's existence, and (c) this evidence is discoverable not simply in principle, but in practice. To be sure, some theistic noninferentialists also believe there is inferential probabilifying evidence of God's existence; and, as stated in Chapter 1, one may be at once a theistic inferentialist and a theistic noninferentialist. But theistic noninferentialists are conceptually distinct from theistic inferentialists and their position should be evaluated as such.

Theistic noninferentialists face a problem that is similar to, but distinct from, the problem theistic inferentialists face—one that I refer to as the "problem of the hiddenness of God."[1] It is as follows—if there is discoverable noninferential probabilifying evidence of God's existence, why is this evidence so scarcely apprehended, if it is apprehended at all? Consider William Alston's and Richard Swinburne's experiences of God. Only a very small percentage of human beings have ever claimed to have had such experiences. Indeed, even if Swinburne's assertion that "millions and millions" of us have claimed to have had such experiences is true, that leaves *billions and billions* of us who have not made such a claim. For the vast majority of us, it is as if God is hiding, if he even exists (merely *claiming* to have had such an experience, after all, does not entail that one actually had one or that the experience was veridical). Hence, Nicholas Everitt's observation that it is "very rare to find reports of anyone who is converted to theism from a position of agnosticism or atheism purely on the basis of religious experiences."[2]

---

[1] As stated in Chapter 1, though I raise the problem of the hiddenness of God here with respect to noninferential evidence, it can be and has been raised with respect to inferential evidence as well. See, for example, J. L. Schellenberg's (1993), *Divine Hiddenness and Human Reason*. Ithaca, NY: Cornell University Press.

[2] Nicholas Everitt (2009), *The Non-existence of God*. London: Routledge, 150.

There are a number of possible solutions to the problem of the hiddenness of God. But they all seem to boil down to the following—if God were not hidden, humans would be coerced into or otherwise begin thinking and/or behaving in ways deemed undesirable by God.[3] This brings us to one of the most popular solutions to the problem of the hiddenness of God—God's hiddenness is necessary if we are to have morally significant freedom and, with it, the ability to develop morally significant characters. A solution along these lines is commonly referred to as a "soul-making" defense of God's hiddenness. In what follows, I address this solution, arguing that it not only fails to adequately solve the problem of the hiddenness of God, it gives us reason to believe that God does not exist. Before doing so, however, a closer look at the problem of the hiddenness of God is in order.

The problem of the hiddenness of God

J. L. Schellenberg, a foremost proponent of the problem of the hiddenness of God, understands the hiddenness of God as "the absence of some kind of positive experiential result in the search for God."[4] At first glance, one might wonder what is so problematic about the absence of a positive experiential result in the search for God. Schellenberg motivates what is so problematic about it by way of the following analogy:

> Imagine yourself in the following situation. You're a child playing hide-and-seek with your mother in the woods at the back of your house. You've been crouching for some time now behind a large oak tree, quite a fine hiding place but not undiscoverable—certainly not for someone as clever as your mother. However, she does not appear. The sun is setting, and it will soon be bedtime, but still no mother. Not only isn't she finding you, but, more disconcerting, you can't hear her anymore: she's not beating the nearby bushes, making those exaggerated "looking for you" noises, and talking to you meanwhile as mothers playing this game usually do. Now imagine that you start calling for your mother. Coming out from behind the tree, you yell out her name, over and over again. "Mooooommmmm!" But no answer. You look everywhere: through the woods, in the house, down the road. An hour passes, and you are growing hoarse from calling. Is she around? Would she fail to answer if she were around?[5]

Of course not, Schellenberg maintains—at least, not if she is a good mother and capable of answering you.

---

[3] See Daniel Howard-Snyder and Paul K. Moser (2002), "Introduction," In Daniel Howard-Snyder and Paul K. Moser (eds), *Divine Hiddenness: New Essays*. Cambridge: Cambridge University Press, 9–10.

[4] J. L. Schellenberg (2004), "Does Divine Hiddenness Justify Atheism?," In Michael L. Peterson and Raymond J. VanArragon (eds), *Contemporary Debates in Philosophy of Religion*. Oxford: Blackwell Publishing, 31.

[5] Ibid., 31.

Schellenberg goes on to modify the analogy in various ways—now you're a child with amnesia who is unsure if your mother even exists, and so on—but the original analogy sets up the problem of God's hiddenness rather well. For, first, it captures many of the significant aspects of the problem of hiddenness, including that someone is hidden (in this case, your mother) as well as the intellectual and emotional turmoil that, after much investigation, may result from one's being confronted with such hiddenness. Second, it captures the relevance and importance of hiddenness with respect to noninferential evidence. To be sure, Schellenberg begins motivating the problem of your mother's hiddenness by invoking instances of hiddenness with respect to *inferential* evidence—"you can't hear her anymore: she's not beating the nearby bushes, making those exaggerated 'looking for you' noises . . ." But then, he invokes instances of hiddenness with respect to *noninferential* evidence—in particular, direct perception—of your mother—"Coming out from behind the tree . . . You look everywhere: through the woods, in the house, down the road."

With this analogy in mind, Schellenberg then has us consider someone else often sought after but not found—God. As an omniscient, omnipotent, perfectly good being, God would not fail to answer the cries of those who seek him in sincerity or anyone else who would be in a loving relationship with him if he existed. He would not, in other words, allow for there to be instances of what Schellenberg calls "nonresistant nonbelief"—instances of people who are open to being in a loving relationship with God but, through no fault of their own, fail to apprehend noninferential (or inferential, for that matter) probabilifying evidence of his existence.[6] Yet, there *are* instances of nonresistant nonbelief. As Schellenberg writes:

> Consider, for example, those who have always believed in God and who would love to go on believing in God but who have found, as adults, that serious and honest examination of all the evidence of experience and argument they can lay their hands on has unexpectedly had the result of eroding their belief away. These are individuals who were happy and morally committed believers and who remain morally committed but are no longer happy because of the emotional effects of an intellectual reorganization involving the removal of theistic belief . . . Consider also all those—both at the present time and throughout the past— in whom theistic belief has never been a live option. In some such individuals, quite other beliefs, supported by authority or tradition or experience, have held sway instead of theism. In others, the basic conceptual conditions of so much as entertaining the idea of a being separate from a created physical universe who is all-powerful, all-knowing, and perfectly good and loving in relation to it have never been satisfied.[7]

From instances of nonresistant nonbelief such as these, Schellenberg infers that God does not exist. He summarizes his argument as follows:

---

[6] Schellenberg (2007), *The Wisdom to Doubt*. Ithaca, NY: Cornell University Press, 205.
[7] Ibid., 205.

P1: Necessarily, if God exists, anyone who is (a) not resisting God and (b) capable of meaningful conscious relationship with God is also (c) in a position to participate in such relationship (able to do so by trying).

P2: Necessarily, one is at a time in a position to participate in meaningful conscious relationship with God only if at that time one believes that God exists.

P3: Necessarily, if God exists, anyone who is (a) not resisting God and (b) capable of meaningful conscious relationship with God also (c) believes that God exists.

P4: There are (and often have been) people who are (a) not resisting God and (b) capable of meaningful conscious relationship with God *without* also (c) believing that God exists.

C: God does not exist.[8]

The soul-making defense of God's hiddenness

Having looked at the problem of the hiddenness of God a little more closely, let us now consider one of the most popular solutions to it—the soul-making defense. Soul-making defenses of God's hiddenness have been offered by a number of theistic philosophers, such as John Hick, Richard Swinburne, and Laura L. Garcia.[9] But one of the clearest and most powerful articulations of it is Michael J. Murray's. It may be summarized in the following way.

First, having morally significant freedom and, with it, the ability to develop morally significant characters is a (very) good thing. As a result, God desires that we have morally significant freedom and has given it to us. The causal relation between having morally significant freedom and having the ability to develop morally significant characters is understood roughly as follows. If one freely chooses to do that which is morally right, then one is responsible for doing that which is morally right. In turn, one becomes a morally good—or, at least, morally better—person. If one freely chooses to do that which is morally wrong, then one is responsible for doing that which is morally wrong. In turn, one becomes a morally bad—or, at least, morally worse—person. And, if one freely chooses to do that which is neither morally right nor morally wrong—that is, if one freely chooses to do that which is morally neutral—then one is responsible for doing that which is morally neutral. In turn, one becomes neither a morally good (better) nor a morally bad (worse) person. (For simplicity's sake, I will write hereafter simply of becoming a morally better or morally worse person.)

Second, there is a correlative relationship between morality and God's commands—that which is morally right is correlative to what God has commanded us to do, and that which is morally wrong is correlative to what God has commanded us not to do. The correlation may hold because God's commands are rooted in knowledge of which acts are morally right and which are morally wrong; or, it may hold because

---

[8] Ibid., 204–6.
[9] John Hick (1966), *Evil and the Love of God*. New York, NY: Harper and Row, 207–400; Richard Swinburne (1979), *The Existence of God*. Oxford: Clarendon Press, 211–12; Laura L. Garcia, "St. John of the Cross and the Necessity of Divine Hiddenness," in *Divine Hiddenness: New Essays*, 83–97.

God's commands *make* acts morally right and morally wrong. In any case, there is a correlative relationship between morality and God's commands.

Third, God is pleased with those who freely obey his commands—with those who freely choose to do that which is morally right—and rewards them with eternal bliss. And God is displeased with those who freely disobey his commands—with those who freely choose to do that which is morally wrong—and punishes them with eternal damnation. Exactly how often one must freely obey or disobey God's commands such that one deserves eternal bliss or eternal damnation is unclear. Suffice it to say that, at the end of our earthly lives, God rewards some of us with eternal bliss for freely obeying his commands and punishes some of us with eternal damnation for freely disobeying his commands.[10]

Finally, if God were not hidden, then we would be aware of what God has commanded us to do as well as what he has commanded us not to do; that is, we would be aware of which acts are morally right and which are morally wrong. We would also be aware of the respective consequences of obedience and disobedience to his commands. As a result, we—at least, and importantly, *some* of us—would strongly desire to choose to do that which is morally right and to refrain from doing that which is morally wrong in an attempt to obtain eternal bliss and avoid eternal damnation.[11] Our strong desire to choose to do that which is morally right and to refrain from doing that which is morally wrong would be sufficiently compelling to render every other course of action unreasonable for us. In short, if God were not hidden, we would be coerced into doing that which is morally right and refraining from doing that which is morally wrong. In turn, we would lose morally significant freedom and, with it, the ability to develop morally significant characters. For, when one does something as a result of *coercion* (divine or otherwise), one is not responsible for doing it; and when one is not responsible for doing something, one does not become a morally better or morally worse person for doing it. Thus, if God were not hidden, we would not have the ability to become morally better or morally worse persons, much less persons deserving of eternal bliss or eternal damnation. But, again, having the ability to develop morally significant characters is a (very) good thing and, as such, something God desires for us. Consequently, God is—indeed, must be—hidden.

The soul-making defense of God's hiddenness, then, may be summarized as follows:

P1: We have the ability to develop morally significant characters.
P2: If God exists and is not hidden, then we do not have the ability to develop morally significant characters.[12]
C: God exists and is hidden.

[10] Michael J. Murray, "Deus Absconditus," in *Divine Hiddenness: New Essays*, 67.
[11] Ibid., 67 and 75.
[12] For practical purposes, I have chosen to state P2 as an indicative conditional rather than as a subjunctive or counterfactual conditional, though there is no major difference between the two since, in this case, we are dealing with present-tense conditionals. As Graham Priest states, there is no major difference between "If I shoot you, you will die" and "If I were to shoot you, you would die." See Graham Priest (2001), *An Introduction to Non-Classical Logic*. Cambridge: Cambridge University Press, 12.

First objection: From God's hiddenness to God's nonexistence

The soul-making defense of God's hiddenness is subject to a number of objections; indeed, too many to present here.[13] For the sake of space, I shall present just three. One objection is that, ironically, it gives us reason to believe that God does not exist. I begin with this objection.

Though being coerced may be one way to lose the ability to develop morally significant characters, it is certainly not the only way. Another way to lose the ability to develop morally significant characters is through inculpable ignorance of the moral status of actions, or so I shall argue. I shall also argue that, for some people, there is a direct line from God's hiddenness to inculpable ignorance of the moral status of actions and, with it, loss of the ability to develop morally significant characters. From this, the nonexistence of God may be inferred.

Let us begin with losing the ability to develop morally significant characters through inculpable ignorance of the moral status of actions. Consider Smith, who freely and consistently chooses acts that are in fact morally right; yet, he erroneously and inculpably believes he is choosing acts that are morally neutral.[14] Is Smith a morally better person in virtue of freely and consistently choosing acts that are morally right? It seems not. And, why not? Because he does not *intend* to choose acts that are morally right. And he does not intend to do so because he is inculpably ignorant of the fact that they *are* morally right. It seems, then, that Smith is a morally better person only if he intends to choose acts that are, in fact, morally right. And he cannot intend to choose acts that are morally right if he is inculpably ignorant of the moral status of the acts he chooses.

Similarly, consider Jones, who freely and consistently chooses acts that are, in fact, morally wrong; yet, she erroneously and inculpably believes she is choosing acts that are morally neutral. Is Jones a morally worse person in virtue of freely and consistently choosing acts that are morally wrong? It seems not. And, why not? Because she does not *intend* to choose acts that are morally wrong. And she does not intend to do so because she is inculpably ignorant of the fact that they *are* morally wrong. It seems, then, that Jones is a morally worse person only if she intends to choose acts that are, in fact, morally wrong. And she cannot intend to choose acts that are morally wrong if she is inculpably ignorant of the moral status of the acts she chooses.

If the preceding is correct, then, in addition to the condition that soul-making defenders deem necessary for the development of morally significant characters—

---

[13] Additional objections to the soul-making defense of God's hiddenness include—Do we *really* have morally significant freedom? Is morally significant freedom *really* required for the ability to develop morally significant characters? Why *must* God punish those who disobey his commands, let alone punish them with eternal damnation? For other objections, see Schellenberg's *Divine Hiddenness and Human Reason* and *The Wisdom to Doubt*.

[14] Most moral theories allow for the possibility of doing that which is, in fact, morally right while not intending to do so. That said, for present purposes, I will grant that there may be a moral theory in which this is not possible.

morally significant freedom—we need to add a second necessary condition—that we intend to choose acts that are, in fact, morally right or morally wrong. (Murray, incidentally, seems to agree.)[15] And intending to choose acts that are morally right or morally wrong cannot be done if we are inculpably ignorant of the moral status of actions.

This brings us to the direct line from God's hiddenness to inculpable ignorance of the moral status of actions and, with it, loss of the ability to develop morally significant characters. Due to God's hiddenness, some people reject belief in God's existence through no fault of their own, such as Schellenberg's nonresistant nonbelievers. As a result, some of these people become moral nihilists. For they believe that if God does not exist, moral nihilism is true. If there is a phrase that captures their position succinctly, it is "If God does not exist, all is permitted."[16] As moral nihilists, they do not believe that morally right and morally wrong acts exist. Accordingly, when these atheists-turned-moral nihilists choose an act, they do not intend to choose one that is morally right or morally wrong since they do not believe that acts *can be* morally right or morally wrong. But, since intending to choose acts that are morally right or morally wrong is a necessary condition for having the ability to develop morally significant characters, these atheists-turned-moral nihilists are not able to develop morally significant characters. That is, they are not able to become morally better or morally worse persons, much less persons deserving of eternal bliss or eternal damnation.

(This is the case, of course, even if moral nihilism is false and some acts are, in fact, morally right and morally wrong. When these atheists-turned-moral nihilists choose an act that they erroneously and inculpably believe is morally neutral—though, as a matter of fact, it is morally right—they do not become morally better persons. In order to become morally better persons, they must intend to choose morally right acts. But, as moral nihilists, they do not—indeed, cannot (logically speaking)—do this. And so it is, *mutatis mutandis*, when these atheists-turned-moral nihilists choose an act that they erroneously and inculpably believe is morally neutral, though as a matter of fact, it is morally wrong.)

Due to God's hiddenness, then, some people reject belief in God's existence through no fault of their own and, in turn, embrace moral nihilism. In doing so, they are inculpably ignorant of the fact that some acts are morally right and some are morally wrong. Accordingly, they do not intend to choose morally right or morally wrong acts. As a result, they are not able to develop morally significant characters since a necessary condition for the development of morally significant characters is that one intend to choose morally right or morally wrong acts. In short, if God exists and is hidden,

---

[15] While discussing a case of inculpable ignorance of the consequences of firing a gun at someone, Murray states that "it seems clear that one could not be said to be morally responsible for their actions if they had no way of knowing that their undertaking, in this case firing the gun, would have the undesirable consequence of taking another life" (Michael J. Murray (1993), "Coercion and the Hiddenness of God," *American Philosophical Quarterly* 30(1): 29).

[16] See Jean Paul Sartre (1975), "Existentialism is a Humanism," In Walter Kaufmann (ed.), *Existentialism from Dostoevsky to Sartre*. New York, NY: New American Library, 353.

then we—again, at least some of us—lose our ability to develop morally significant characters through inculpable ignorance of the moral status of actions. Thus,

P3: If God exists and is hidden, then we do not have the ability to develop morally significant characters.

If the preceding is correct, then God's hiddenness is no more compatible with our ability to develop morally significant characters than is his unhiddenness. For, if God exists, he is either hidden or not hidden and, either way, we do not have the ability to develop morally significant characters. But, we do have the ability to develop morally significant characters, or so soul-making defenders of God's hiddenness believe. So, given their own reasoning, God does not exist. To see this more clearly, consider the following:

P1: We have the ability to develop morally significant characters.
P2: If God exists and is not hidden, then we do not have the ability to develop morally significant characters.
P3: If God exists and is hidden, then we do not have the ability to develop morally significant characters.
P4: If God exists, then either he exists and is hidden, or he exists and is not hidden. (Tautology)
P5: God exists and is not hidden. (Assumption)
C1: We do not have the ability to develop morally significant characters.
C2: We have the ability to develop morally significant characters and we do not have the ability to develop morally significant characters.
C3: It is not the case that God exists and is not hidden. (Reductio: P5–C2)
P6: God exists and is hidden. (Assumption)
C4: We do not have the ability to develop morally significant characters.
C5: We have the ability to develop morally significant characters and we do not have the ability to develop morally significant characters.
C6: It is not the case that God exists and is hidden. (Reductio: P6–C5)
C7: It is not the case that God exists and is not hidden *and* it is not the case that God exists and is hidden.
C8: God does not exist.

Possible replies

Given the validity of the preceding argument for the nonexistence of God, if one is to defeat it, one must reject either P1, P2, P3, or P4. Soul-making defenders of God's hiddenness will be loath to reject P1 and P2, of course. And no one would—at least, *should*—reject P4 as it is a tautology. So, let us focus on P3. I have already provided a defense of it, of course, but perhaps there are criticisms of it such that, all things considered, it is more likely to be false than true.

Do atheists-turned-moral nihilists really exist?

Obviously, P3 depends upon the claim that some people reject belief in God's existence and become moral nihilists. But is this true? Do atheists-turned-moral nihilists really exist? There seems to be only one source from which we could derive an accurate answer to this question—those who claim to be them. They, more than anyone else, would know whether they *really are* atheists-turned-moral nihilists. So, do some people claim to be atheists-turned-moral nihilists? They do, one of the most famous examples of which is Jean Paul Sartre. In his "Existentialism Is a Humanism," Sartre states:

> Dostoevsky once wrote: "If God did not exist, everything would be permitted" . . . Everything is indeed permitted if God does not exist, and man is in consequence forlorn, for he cannot find anything to depend upon either within or outside himself. He discovers forthwith, that he is without excuse. For if indeed existence precedes essence, one will never be able to explain one's action by reference to a given and specific human nature; in other words, there is no determinism— man is free, man *is* freedom. Nor, on the other hand, if God does not exist, are we provided with any values or commands that could legitimize our behavior. Thus we have neither behind us, nor before us in a luminous realm of values, any means of justification or excuse.[17]

To be sure, this passage addresses more than Sartre's understanding of the relation between God's existence and morality. But, one thing it makes clear is that, for Sartre, there is a direct line from God's nonexistence to moral nihilism.

Or, for a more recent example, consider another philosopher, Joel Marks. After critically reflecting upon the relation between his atheism and morality, Marks "saw no escape from moral nihilism."[18] Accordingly, he proposes that we reject the view that we have the ability to develop morally significant characters. As he puts it,

> My proposal is that we abandon moral concepts, attitudes and language. This means, in concrete terms, no more seeking or demanding moral justifications, no more experiencing or trying to instill moral guilt, no more assuming or assigning moral responsibility, no more assessing moral desert or exacting just retribution, etc.[19]

As with Sartre, for Marks, there is a direct line from God's nonexistence to moral nihilism. These are just two examples of atheists-turned-moral nihilists, but it stands to reason there are many more.

To be sure, merely claiming that one is an atheist-turned-moral nihilist does not immediately entail that one really is one. Even so, unless we have good reason to doubt their testimony, it seems we should take them at their word, just as we take people

---

[17] Ibid., 353.
[18] http://opinionator.blogs.nytimes.com/2011/08/21/confessions-of-an-ex-moralist/.
[19] http://opinionator.blogs.nytimes.com/2011/09/02/atheism-amorality-and-animals-a-response/.

who claim to be theists or agnostics at their word. Some might think that the behavior of these atheists-turned-moral nihilists could be good reason to doubt whether they really are what they claim to be. After all, if they do not behave like atheists-turned-moral nihilists, they may not be them. But this will not suffice—at least, not in every case—since one's behavior need not always correspond to one's beliefs. Due to weakness of the will, misinformation, confusion, or other factors, one can believe something, X, while engaging in behavior more consistent with someone who believes not-X.

The depth and breadth of the loss

Another way to reject P3 is to find a disanalogy between losing the ability to develop morally significant characters through divine coercion, on the one hand, and losing the ability to develop morally significant characters through inculpable ignorance of the moral status of actions, on the other. For example, one might argue that, in the case of losing the ability to develop morally significant characters through divine coercion, the loss is absolute and pervasive—absolute, in that divinely coerced individuals *never* have the opportunity to develop morally significant characters; and pervasive, in that *many* individuals lose the ability to develop morally significant characters. While, in the case of losing the ability to develop morally significant characters through inculpable ignorance of the moral status of actions, the loss is neither absolute nor pervasive—not absolute, in that atheists-turned-moral nihilists *sometimes* have the opportunity to develop morally significant characters; and not pervasive, in that *not* many individuals lose the ability to develop morally significant characters in this way. Let us consider each of these possible disanalogies.

Beginning with the breadth of the loss, it may indeed be that more individuals lose the ability to develop morally significant characters if God is not hidden than if God is hidden. Then again, it may not be. In any case, however, such hypothesizing is irrelevant. Even Murray concedes that not *everyone* loses the ability to develop morally significant characters if God is not hidden, only some of us do. "Making us powerfully aware of the truth of God's existence," he writes, "would suffice to coerce (at least many of) us into behaving in accordance with God's moral commands."[20] Not only does "(at least many of) us" suggest that not all of us would be so coerced, it entails neither that all nor even that the majority of us would be. And it is in virtue of *that* fact—that just *some* of us would lose the ability to develop morally significant characters—that God allegedly must be hidden. As Murray writes, "God would want such self-determination to be available to *all* free creatures, not merely some."[21]

As for the depth of the loss, one might argue that atheists-turned-moral nihilists sometimes have the opportunity to develop morally significant characters on the grounds that there are times at which they are either *culpably* ignorant of the moral status of actions or *not ignorant* of the moral status of actions. But that this is so isn't

---

[20] Murray, "Deus Absconditus," 63, emphasis mine.
[21] Ibid., 77.

clear. So long as atheists-turned-moral nihilists find their views to be more reasonable than the alternatives, the most reasonable thing for them to do is to think in terms of atheism and moral nihilism and behave accordingly. Granted, it is unlikely that atheists-turned-moral nihilists will always choose to do that which is most reasonable. But it is also unlikely that potentially divinely coerced individuals will always choose to do that which is most reasonable. Even Murray concedes this, as indicated above. (And, if the stories the Old and New Testaments are any indication, it is rather likely that individuals won't always obey God's commands; indeed, many will find it difficult to do so.) All this to say, if the likelihood of always choosing to do that which is most reasonable counts against the depth of the loss of atheists-turned-moral nihilists, it should count equally against the depth of the loss of potentially divinely coerced individuals.

Finally, that the loss of the ability to develop morally significant characters through divine coercion is absolute depends upon the assumption that obeying God's commands in an attempt to obtain eternal bliss and avoid eternal damnation is the *only* reasonable course of action. But this is doubtful, for two reasons. First, whether a course of action is reasonable is, at some level, if not fundamentally, person-relative. Second, and related to the previous point, there is reason to think that, for some people, disobeying God's commands is not only reasonable but, in some cases, more reasonable than obeying God's commands, even if their disobedience results in the loss of eternal bliss and the procurement of eternal damnation. I will discuss these things in turn.

On reasonable alternatives to obeying God's commands

When is a course of action reasonable? To answer this, let us begin with an example Murray provides regarding reasonable and unreasonable courses of action.[22] Murray asks us to consider someone who threatens to shoot him if he does not hand over his money. In such a situation, Murray claims, it is impossible for him reasonably to take any other course of action except that of handing over his money. In other words, every other course of action, save for handing over the money, is unreasonable.

Granted, it may be impossible for *Murray* reasonably to take any other course of action except that of handing over the money. But, this need not be the case for everyone. Most philosophers maintain that what makes a course of action reasonable is a function, at some level if not fundamentally, of the actor's desires, interests, and needs, among other things. (Murray, once again, seems to agree.)[23] If this is correct, then what makes handing over the money the only reasonable course of action is a function of Murray's desires, interests, needs, etc. Two of Murray's desires, for example, are to retain his money and to retain his bodily integrity, with the latter being the stronger of the two. But, not everyone's desires, interests, and needs will be—or even ought to be—identical to Murray's. For some people, it may be that handing over the

---

[22] Ibid., 70.
[23] While explaining why he would hand over the money, Murray states that he would do so "since I care a great deal about my bodily integrity, far more than keeping the few dollars I carry with me" (Ibid., 70).

money is *not* the only reasonable course of action to take or even *a* reasonable course of action. Consider, for example, someone who does not desire to retain his bodily integrity, or someone whose desire to retain his bodily integrity is not the *strongest* of his desires—someone whose strongest desire is to thwart criminal activity or to find compromises in such situations. For such individuals, it is not the case that the only reasonable course of action to take is that of handing over the money.[24] All this to say, what is reasonable for Murray to do need not be what is reasonable for someone else to do.

This brings us to the second point—there is reason to think that, for some people, disobeying God's commands may not only be reasonable, but more reasonable than obeying them, even if their disobedience results in the loss of eternal bliss and the procurement of eternal damnation.

For instance, God's commands are often found to be objectionable in the extreme. Just consider the following commands, taken from the Old Testament:

He who strikes his father or his mother shall surely be put to death. (Exodus 21:15)

He who curses his father or his mother shall surely be put to death. (Exodus 21:17)

If there is a man who commits adultery with another man's wife, one who commits adultery with his friend's wife, the adulterer and the adulteress shall surely be put to death. (Leviticus 20:10)

If there is a man who lies with a male as those who lie with a woman, both of them have committed a detestable act; they shall surely be put to death. Their bloodguiltiness is upon them. (Leviticus 20:13)

If there is a man who lies with an animal, he shall surely be put to death; you shall also kill the animal. (Leviticus 20:16)

Moreover, the one who blasphemes the name of the Lord shall surely be put to death; all the congregation shall certainly stone him. The alien as well as the native, when he blasphemes the Name, shall be put to death. (Leviticus 24:16)

---

[24] Of course, Murray may think that it is unreasonable for someone not to desire to retain his bodily integrity, or for the desire to retain his bodily integrity not to be the strongest of his desires. But a claim about which *desires* are reasonable is neither here nor there, since it is claims about which *courses of action* are reasonable that are at work in his defense of the hiddenness of God, not which *desires* are reasonable. But, even if claims about which desires are reasonable were at work as well, a question arises—what makes a desire reasonable? As mentioned above, what makes a course of action reasonable is a function of the actor's desires, interests, and needs, among other things—the desires, interests, and needs constitute the backdrop against which the reasonableness of a course of action is determined. What, then, constitutes the backdrop against which the reasonableness of a desire is determined? Either there is a backdrop or there is not and, either way, there are problems. For, if there is a backdrop, a similar problem arises—what is the backdrop against which the reasonableness of *this* backdrop is determined? An infinite regress lurks. If, on the other hand, there is no backdrop against which the reasonableness of a desire is determined, then it is either a brute fact that the desire is reasonable or it is neither reasonable nor unreasonable. In any of these cases, the view that it is unreasonable for someone not to desire to retain one's bodily integrity, or for the desire to retain one's bodily integrity not to be the strongest of one's desires, faces challenges.

If two men, a man and his countryman, are struggling together, and the wife of one comes near to deliver her husband from the hand of the one who is striking him, and puts out her hand and seizes his genitals, then you shall cut off her hand; you shall not show pity. (Deuteronomy 25:11–12)[25]

Many people find such commands to be so objectionable that disobedience to them is a reasonable, if not more reasonable, alternative to obedience, even if disobedience results in the loss of eternal bliss and the procurement of eternal damnation. Following John Stuart Mill's lead, these people hold that if a god who commands these objectionable acts can sentence them to eternal damnation for disobeying his commands, then to eternal damnation they will go.[26]

Of course, one might argue that God would not command such acts on the grounds that each is immoral. But, in the present context, such a reply is problematic—God's not commanding such acts due to their immorality is difficult to reconcile with the view that God damns eternally those who disobey his commands. To see this, consider the command regarding killing a parent-cursing child. Presumably, killing a parent-cursing child is immoral in virtue of its injustice (among other things)—the child does not deserve to be killed for cursing his parents. According to the reply under consideration, since killing the child is unjust and thereby immoral, God would not command it. With this in mind, we might ask whether one who disobeys God's commands to one extent or another *deserves* to be eternally damned. Many theistic and nontheistic philosophers alike believe one does not deserve this, that imposing such a punishment would be unjust and thereby immoral.[27] If this is correct, and if God would not command immoral acts, then, *a fortiori*, God would not *engage* in the immoral act of imposing this punishment on one who disobeys his commands.

What's more, if God would not damn eternally those who disobey his commands, then the soul-making defense of God's hiddenness is undermined. For, according to it, our fear of eternal damnation (among other things) would coerce us into obeying God's commands. But if we have reason to believe that God would not damn us eternally, then we have reason to reject the claim that we would be coerced through fear of eternal damnation.[28]

Another reason for thinking that there are reasonable alternatives to obeying some of God's commands is that God is allegedly mysterious—"his ways are not our ways," as some theists put it. Based on God's mysterious nature, it may be reasonable to believe that the alleged correlative relationship between morality and God's commands does not always hold. Specifically, it may be reasonable to hold that, in some cases, rather

---

[25] For a more extensive catalogue of seriously problematic commands of God, see Elizabeth Anderson (2007), "If God is Dead, Is Everything Permitted?", In Louise M. Antony (ed.), *Philosophers without Gods: Meditations on Atheism and the Secular Life*. Oxford: Oxford University Press, 218ff.

[26] See John Stuart Mill (1963), *The Collected Works of John Stuart Mill*, Vol. 9, ed. J. M. Robson. Toronto: University of Toronto Press, 103.

[27] See Thomas Talbott, "No Hell," in *Contemporary Debates in Philosophy of Religion*, 278–87.

[28] Of course, one may argue that those who disobey God's commands to one extent or another *do* deserve eternal damnation. I find this view to be implausible and, for that reason and others, I will not address it here.

than commanding us to do that which is morally right, God commands us to do that which is morally wrong in order to test our ability to refrain from immorality—that is, in order to test our moral integrity. Not fulfilling God's commands through disobedience would be a reasonable alternative to obedience in such cases.

One might respond to this in one of two ways. First, one might claim that God's mysterious nature isn't *so* mysterious such that his commands would be interpretively flexible when revealed through unhiddenness. But what reason might one have for believing this? It is certainly not true *a priori*. And one cannot claim to have first-person experience to support such a claim—remember, God is supposed to be (nay, *must* be) hidden. Nor can one rely upon the accounts of Moses, Abraham, and others to whom God has allegedly submitted commands. For either God's commanding them was done when he was not hidden, which flies in the face of the claim that God must be hidden. Or, it was done when he was hidden and, thus, will not serve as sufficient evidence for claims about the interpretive flexibility of God's commands when he is not hidden. That God's mysterious nature isn't so mysterious such that his commands would be interpretively flexible when revealed through unhiddenness, then, is unfounded.

Second, one might respond by denying that God is mysterious. Hardly any theistic philosopher would resort to this response, however. Indeed, for many theistic philosophers, God's mysterious nature serves as a cherished argumentative trump card.

Moreover, whether someone or something is mysterious is person-relative to some extent. I might find the idea that some infinite sets are larger than others to be mysterious, for example, while the set theorist Georg Cantor may not. And it would be odd, if not misguided, to say that one of us is incorrect, that there is an objective truth to the matter. Instead, it seems more accurate to say that whether the idea that some infinite sets are larger than others is mysterious is person-relative to some extent. In this vein, whether God is mysterious may be person-relative to some extent.[29] If this is correct, then even if some people would deny that God is mysterious, others may accept that he is without contradiction. And, the latter may reasonably believe that, at times, this mysterious God commands us to do that which is morally wrong in order to test our moral integrity. For them, disobedience to God's command would be a reasonable alternative to obedience.

To sum up, Murray assumes that we would not have reasonable alternatives to obeying God's commands when he is not hidden. Given what I have argued above, this claim is much less plausible than it may have first appeared.

Second objection: Ways of hiding

My first objection to the soul-making defense of God's hiddenness was that, even if God is hidden, some of us lose our ability to develop morally significant characters through

---

[29] Indeed, presumably God does not find himself to be mysterious, while others do.

inculpable ignorance of the moral status of actions and, thus, the soul-making defense of God's hiddenness gives us reason to believe that God does not exist. This brings us to my second objection, an objection directed at one of the soul-making defense's claims—if God were not hidden, then we would be aware not only of his existence, but of what he has commanded us to do, what he has commanded us not to do, and what the punishments and rewards for disobedience and obedience will be. The assumption here is that God cannot be unhidden with respect to his *existence* while, at the same time, be hidden with respect to his *commands, rewards,* and *punishments.* That is, God cannot make his existence known through unhiddenness without simultaneously making (all of) his commands, punishments, and rewards known through unhiddenness as well.

Now, the problem of the hiddenness of God pertains only to the first of these three things—it pertains only to hiddenness and unhiddenness with respect to God's existence. This is due to the fact that belief in God's existence is, in Schellenberg's words,

> obviously and necessarily one of the conditions of being in a position to exercise one's capacity for meaningful conscious relationship with God—how can I experience nature as the creature of God or hear God speak to me (interpreting it as God speaking) or consciously experience Divine forgiveness and support or feel grateful to God or experience God's loving and inspiring presence and respond thereto in love and obedience and worship if I do not believe that there is a God?[30]

Yet—and here's the rub—it is logically possible for God to be unhidden in this first respect while, at the same time, be hidden in the second and third respects. There is no contradiction in the conception of God making his existence known to us through unhiddenness without simultaneously making (all of) his commands, punishments, and rewards known to us through unhiddenness as well. And, if it is logically possible for God not to be hidden with respect to his existence while remaining hidden with respect to his commands, rewards, and punishments, then it is simply not the case that God must remain hidden in order for soul-making to take place.[31]

A few objections may be raised at this point. We begin with one from Murray. Murray argues that, given God's loving nature, he would not make his existence known to us through unhiddenness without simultaneously making (all of) his commands, punishments, and rewards known to us through unhiddenness as well. As he puts it:

---

[30] Schellenberg, *The Wisdom to Doubt,* 204.
[31] To motivate this beyond mere logical possibility, suppose intelligent extraterrestrials exist and have the technology to reach Earth. These extraterrestrials could make their existence known to us without simultaneously making all of their beliefs, desires, and the behavior that might stem from them known to us. They could do this simply by, say, hovering over various cities in their spaceships (à la the film *Independence Day*). Or, to use an example closer to home, *we* can make our existence known to others without simultaneously making all of our beliefs, desires, and the behavior that might stem from them known to others. We can do this, for example, by merely placing ourselves in the presence of others. And, if we and the extraterrestrials can make our existence known to others without simultaneously making all of our beliefs, desires, and the behavior that might stem from them known to others, God can do the divine equivalent of this, whatever that may be like.

One might . . . agree that God would make his existence plainly known, but might argue further that God's loving nature further entails that other facts would be made known as well. Many theists claim that ultimate human fulfillment requires not only belief in God, but a number of other beliefs about what it takes to be rightly related to God as well. If loving entails seeking the well-being of the beloved, God would surely seek to make the necessary information for fulfillment available. As a result, I will assume for the moment . . . that, all other things being equal, God's love would lead him to make us aware not merely of his bare existence, but also of all the other truths needed to obtain our complete temporal and eternal happiness.[32]

The key clause—for both Murray's argument and my reply to it—is "all other things being equal." To see this, simply ask—if God's loving nature *entails* that he would make us aware of all the other truths needed to obtain our complete temporal and eternal happiness, why aren't we currently aware of all those other truths? Murray's reply, of course, is that not all other things are equal—God also wants us to develop morally significant characters so, all things considered, he hides himself as well as those other truths. But why should Murray's all-things-considered claim be preferred to this one—God wants to make his bare existence known to us so, all things considered, he does not hide himself, but he does hide those other truths, thereby preserving our ability to develop morally significant characters?

Murray has his reasons for preferring his claim to the latter claim. As he writes, "Surely it would not be an act of love of God towards creatures to keep facts about human flourishing tucked safely behind the counter simply in order to make his existence clearly known."[33] This would be all well and good if, in hiding himself, God thereby ensured that facts about human flourishing were clearly known. But, facts about human flourishing—both those that pertain to a relationship with God and those that do not—are not clearly known. Indeed, far from it, as is evidenced by our incessant debating on issues of health, psychology, child rearing, economics, education, morality, politics, art, philosophy, and more. So, as with the above, why should Murray's claim be preferred to this one—surely it would not be an act of love of God toward creatures to keep the fact of his existence tucked safely behind the counter simply to make facts about human flourishing insufficiently known? At best, I submit, we are left with an impasse; at worst, God has tucked the wrong thing behind the counter.

Second, one might object that the reason God cannot make his existence known to us through unhiddenness without simultaneously making (all of) his commands, punishments, and rewards known to us through unhiddenness as well has to do not with God, but with us. Simply put, we would not *recognize* God without knowledge of his commands, punishments, and rewards. But this is implausible—if an omniscient, omnipotent being can do anything, he can make his existence known to us in such a way that would recognize him without putting (all of) his commands, punishments, and

---

[32]　Murray, "Deus Absconditus," 67.
[33]　Ibid., 76.

rewards on full display. Even Alston agrees with this, at least with regard to *perceiving* God. As he writes:

> To perceptually recognize your house, it is not necessary that the object even display features that are *in fact* only possessed by your house, much less features that *only* your house could possess. It is enough that the object present to my experience features that, in this situation or in situations in which I generally find myself, are sufficiently indicative of (are a reliable guide to) the object's being your house. And so it is here. For me to recognize what I am aware of (X) as God, all that is necessary is that X present features that are in fact a reliable indication of their possessor's being God, at least in situations of the sort in which I typically find myself. It is, again, not required that these features attach only to God, still less that they should be such that they can attach only to God.[34]

And if this is the case with perceiving God, I see no reason why this cannot be the case with nonperceptual awareness of God.

Commands, punishments, and rewards aside, there may be another reason why we would not recognize God. One might argue—contra Alston—that it is impossible for us to have an experience of God, as any experience we may have will fail to capture God's essential qualities. As Walter Sinnott-Armstrong puts it, "even if religious experiences were evidence for something, they could not be evidence that their source is all-good and all-powerful. The most vivid religious experience could result from a God who is very powerful and pretty good, so they cannot be evidence for a traditional God."[35] With this view, even if God were not hidden, our experience of him would not result in knowing that *he* exists—at best, it would result in knowing that a very knowledgeable, very powerful, and very good being exists.

This may indeed be the case, but one thing is certain—soul-making defenders of God's hiddenness cannot consistently rely upon such an argument. Their position depends on the claim that some of us would lose the ability to develop morally significant characters as a result of knowing that *God*—an omniscient, omnipotent, perfectly good being—exists. But, given the preceding argument, experiences of God will not result in knowing that God exists; rather, at best, they will result in knowing that a very knowledgeable, very powerful, and very good being exists.

Additionally, if experiences of God will not result in knowing that God exists, then once again the question arises—why is God hidden, if he even exists? For, given this

---

[34] William P. Alston (1991), *Perceiving God: The Epistemology of Religious Experience*. Ithaca, NY: Cornell University Press, 96–7.

[35] Walter Sinnott-Armstrong (2006), "The Argument from Ignorance," In Michael Martin and Ricki Monnier (eds), *The Improbability of God*. Amherst, NY: Prometheus Books, 382. Georges Rey makes a similar point, ". . . ask yourself how local, personal experiences could possibly provide serious evidence for the existence of a *necessary, eternal, omni*-being responsible for *the creation of the world*. How does the presence of such a being feel differently from that of a merely contingent, finitely old and powerful one?" (Georges Rey, "Meta-Atheism: Religious Avowal as Self-Deception," in *Philosophers without Gods*, 249–50) Everitt ups the ante, arguing that God "is not even a possible object of sensory experience" (see Everitt, 172ff).

view, even if God were *not* hidden, we would not lose the ability to develop morally significant characters in virtue of knowing that he exists, since we would not know that *he* exists—we would know simply that a very knowledgeable, very powerful, and very good being exists. What's more, our knowing that a very knowledgeable, very powerful, and very good being exists would be tremendously beneficial, as we would know that we are not alone in the universe, among other things. Indeed, we would have that much more evidence—though, importantly, not *proof*—that God actually exists— something soul-making defenders of God's hiddenness and other theistic philosophers should be the first to welcome. After all, if these theistic philosophers welcome the alleged discovery of a first cause of the universe or designer of the irreducibly complex, they should welcome that much more the discovery of a very knowledgeable, very powerful, and very good being.

Another objection that might be raised is that, were God to make his existence known to us through unhiddenness today, we would know what many of his commands, punishments, and rewards are since we have nearly 2,000 years of Judeo-Christian theology under our belts. But, this just pushes the problem back. For, God could have begun making his existence known to us through unhiddenness from the very beginning—pre-Judeo-Christian theology—and continued to do so through the present without simultaneously making (all of) his commands, punishments, and rewards known to us through unhiddenness as well.[36]

But even if we *would* know what many of his commands, punishments, and rewards are since we have nearly 2,000 years of Judeo-Christian theology under our belts, there remains plenty of room for soul-making. There are many different interpretations of the Bible and, with them, many different understandings of Judeo-Christian theology. Even with the advent and development of Judeo-Christian theology, then, many questions remain unanswered. Accordingly, after making his existence known to us through unhiddenness today, God could refuse to address—explicitly or implicitly— what, exactly, all of his commands are, thereby leaving it up to us to figure them out. Indeed, he is doing an excellent job of that now, if he exists.

Relatedly, there are plenty of actions that are not addressed clearly in the Bible, and there are even more actions that are not addressed at all, explicitly or implicitly. Playing violent video games, lying to your child about his grandmother's imminent death, relying upon in vitro fertilization, undergoing liposuction, assassinating political leaders, watching television, boxing, BDSM, littering—each of these activities is either not addressed clearly in the Bible or not addressed at all. And this list could go on indefinitely. Given this, even if God were no longer hidden and his commands, punishments, and rewards are properly captured by Judeo-Christian theology, there remains plenty of room for soul-making. It is simply not the case, then, that God must be hidden in order for soul-making to take place.

---

[36] This assumes, of course, that God as well as his commands, punishments, and rewards are properly captured by Judeo-Christian theology, an assumption not everyone shares.

Third objection: On intentions, rewards, and punishments

This third and final objection draws from the discussion of my first objection to the soul-making defense of God's hiddenness. Recall, if you will, that my first objection involved the claim that a necessary condition for developing morally significant characters is that we intend to choose acts that are morally right or morally wrong. If one freely chooses to do that which is in fact morally wrong, but does not intend to do so, one does not become a morally worse person through that choice. Similarly, if one freely chooses to do that which is in fact morally right, but does not intend to do so, one does not become a morally better person through that choice.

With this in mind, let us consider the process by which God decides who deserves eternal bliss and who deserves eternal damnation. If God is going to be fair—and he is, given his perfect goodness—he cannot decide simply on the basis of who obeyed his commands and who did not. That is, he cannot decide simply on the basis of who did that which is morally right and who did that which is morally wrong. For, it is one thing to do that which is morally right or morally wrong; it is another thing to *intend* to do that which is morally right or morally wrong. And, as argued above, the latter is a necessary condition for developing morally significant characters—for becoming morally better persons potentially deserving of eternal bliss or morally worse persons potentially deserving of eternal damnation. If God is going to be fair, then, he must decide who deserves eternal bliss and who deserves eternal damnation not simply on the basis of who did that which is morally right and who did that which is morally wrong, but also on the basis of who intended to do that which is morally right and who intended to do that which is morally wrong. In short, if God is going to be fair, he must decide not simply on the basis of *what* people did, but *why* they did it.

Soul-making is possible, then, even if God is not hidden and all of his commands, punishments, and rewards are on full display. For God could also make us aware of the fact that simply doing that which is morally right and refraining from doing that which is morally wrong will not suffice when it comes to deserving eternal bliss and avoiding eternal damnation—we must also *intend* to do that which is morally right and intend to refrain from doing that which is morally wrong. More specifically, he could make us aware of the fact that if one does not *genuinely* intend (to be explained shortly) to do that which is morally right—one's genuine intention is to do that which is morally wrong but, due to God's punishments and rewards, one buckles and does that which is morally right—one does not become a morally better person, much less a person deserving of eternal bliss. In so doing, God would not only make clear, but ensure that soul-making is possible despite his unhiddenness. For God could determine whether one genuinely intended to do that which is morally right or morally wrong, and judge accordingly.

Three objections to the preceding may be raised. First, some might argue that God does not know what our intentions are. But this is simply implausible. God is supposed to be omniscient, and it is all but impossible to believe that his omniscience does not include knowledge of our intentions. Even more problematic, if God does not know what our intentions are, then how can he fairly judge who deserves eternal bliss and who deserves eternal damnation? Again, deciding simply on the basis of who engaged in morally right acts and who engaged in morally wrong acts would be unfair. For one may engage in morally right or morally wrong acts without intending to do so. And, without intending to do so, one does not become a morally better or morally worse person, much less a person deserving of eternal bliss or eternal damnation. If God is to judge us fairly, then, he must know what our intentions are. The soul-making defense of God's hiddenness, then, cannot consistently rely upon the claim that God does not know what our intentions are.

Second, some might argue that the preceding just pushes the problem back—rather than God's unhiddenness coercing us at the level of our actions, God's unhiddenness would coerce us at the level of our intentions. But this is implausible, as an intention that is the product of coercion is not a genuine intention, and only genuine intentions count—at least, *should* count—toward the moral development of one's character. To see this, let us consider again the case of someone who threatens to shoot Murray if he does not hand over his money. Clearly, robbing Murray of his money is immoral, all else being equal; but, just as clearly, Murray is not a morally worse person for handing over his money and thereby participating in the robber's immoral activity. Why not? Because Murray does not genuinely intend to do so. This is perhaps best explained by way of the distinction between first-order and second-order intentions.

First-order intentions are intentions one has regarding anything other than other intentions; while second-order intentions are those that one has regarding one's first-order intentions.[37] And, there is reason to believe that, in order for one's doing something, X, to be one's genuine intention, one's first-order intention must coincide with one's second-order intention—one's first-order intention must be to do X, and one's second-order intention must be to have the first-order intention to do X. Consider, for example, someone who desires to break his addiction to smoking cigarettes. Suppose this would-be quitter is about to smoke a cigarette. In this case, his first-order intention is to smoke a cigarette, but his second-order intention is not to have the first-order intention to smoke a cigarette (after all, he desires to break his addiction to smoking cigarettes). Since his first-order intention does not coincide with his second-order intention, it seems that smoking a cigarette is not his genuine intention. If this is correct, then an intention that is the product of an addiction—of a compulsive physical and/or psychological need—is not a genuine intention.

With the preceding in mind, consider Murray and the robber again. Murray's first-order intention is to hand over the money, but his second-order intention is not to have the first-order intention to hand over the money (he is, after all, being coerced

---

[37] This conceptual distinction is modeled after a similar distinction made by Harry Frankfurt with respect to desires. See Harry Frankfurt (1988), "Freedom of the Will," in *The Importance of What We Care About*, by Harry Frankfurt. New York, NY: Cambridge University Press.

into handing over the money). Since his first-order intention does not coincide with his second-order intention, it seems that handing over the money is not his genuine intention. If this is correct, then an intention that is the product of coercion is not a genuine intention. Accordingly, Murray's handing over the money and thereby participating in the robber's immoral activity does not render him a morally worse person, since only genuine intentions count toward the moral development of one's character.

Similarly, consider someone who is divinely coerced into doing that which is morally right. His first-order intention is to do that which is morally right, but his second-order intention is not to have the first-order intention to do that which is morally right (he is, after all, being coerced into doing that which is morally right). Since his first-order intention does not coincide with his second-order intention, it seems that his doing that which is morally right is not his genuine intention. As a result, his doing that which is morally right does not render him a morally better person—much less a person deserving of eternal bliss—since only genuine intentions count toward the moral development of one's character.

God's making us aware of the fact that we must also intend to do that which is morally right and intend to refrain from doing that which is morally wrong in order to deserve eternal bliss and eternal damnation (respectively) does not push the problem back, then. For God could determine whether one genuinely intended to do that which is morally right or morally wrong, and judge accordingly.

Finally, one might argue that, contrary to what I have supposed, when God decides who deserves eternal bliss and who deserves eternal damnation, he is not required to be fair. But, if this is the case, then the soul-making defense of God's hiddenness is undermined. For, if God is not required to be fair, then we have less reason—if we have reason at all—to believe that obedience to his commands will result in obtaining eternal bliss and avoiding eternal damnation. In turn, the possibilities of obtaining eternal bliss and avoiding eternal damnation are less coercive, if they are coercive at all.

Conclusion

Theistic noninferentialists believe that there is noninferential probabilifying evidence of God's existence. A problem they face—the problem of divine hiddenness—is if there is, why is this evidence so scarcely apprehended, if it is apprehended at all? A popular defense of God's hiddenness—the soul-making defense—is that if God were not hidden, then some of us would lose morally significant freedom and, with it, the ability to develop morally significant characters through divine coercion. In reply, I have argued that:

• if God is hidden, some of us lose our ability to develop morally significant characters through inculpable ignorance of the moral status of actions and, thus, the soul-making defense of God's hiddenness gives us reason to believe that God does not exist,

- it is logically possible for God to be unhidden with respect to his existence while, at the same time, be hidden with respect to his commands, punishments, and rewards, and,
- even if God were not hidden, soul-making would remain possible since God could determine whether one genuinely intended to do that which is morally right or morally wrong and judge accordingly.

If what I have argued is sound, then the soul-making defense of God's hiddenness is simply inadequate.

4

A Problem for Theistic Fideists

Introduction

Thus far, I have presented problems for theistic inferentialists and theistic non-inferentialists. This brings us to theistic fideists, philosophers who believe that (a) God exists, (b) there is no discoverable probabilifying evidence of God's existence, but (c) it is acceptable—morally, if not otherwise—to have faith that God exists.

As with theistic inferentialists and theist noninferentialists, theistic fideists face a problem, one that I refer to as the "problem of faith"—if there is no discoverable probabilifying evidence of God's existence, why think that it is morally acceptable to have faith that he exists? After all, that there is no discoverable probabilifying evidence of God's existence does not immediately entail that having faith that God exists is morally acceptable. Moreover, in many cases, having faith that a belief is true may result in endangering, harming, and/or violating the rights of others. Imagine, for example, a physician who believes that her patient needs a liver transplant, a mechanic who believes his customer's car needs a new engine, a dentist who believes her patient needs a root canal, a lawyer who believes his client should plead guilty, a stockbroker who believes her client should purchase as much stock in Microsoft as possible, and so on. Imagine further that, when asked what evidence they have for their respective beliefs, each replies, "I have not attempted to obtain evidence for my belief and so I do not have any. I have faith that it is true." Clearly, having faith that these beliefs are true may result in endangering, harming, and/or violating the rights of others. In this vein, I argue below that there is at least one condition under which it is *prima facie* wrong to have faith that God exists—when one's belief that God exists will affect others and one has not attempted to believe that God exists on the basis of sufficient evidence. But before presenting my argument, I must first address what I mean by having faith that God exists.

On having faith that God exists

For present purposes, to have faith that God exists is to believe that God exists despite recognizing that one lacks sufficient evidence for believing so. Allow me to explain exactly what I mean by this.

Let us begin with what I mean by "sufficient evidence." As stated in Chapter 1, by "evidence" of God's existence, I mean epistemic reasons for believing that God exists, reasons that indicate the truth of the belief "God exists." This evidence may be inferential, noninferential, public, private, discoverable, undiscovered, and so on. And by "sufficient" evidence, I mean evidence the strength of which is proportional to the strength of the belief derived from it. Simply put, the stronger one believes something, the stronger the evidence must be if it is to be sufficient. Consider two spectrums. For the first spectrum, 1 represents the extreme of belief involving complete certainty, while 0 represents the other extreme of belief involving complete uncertainty. For the second spectrum, 1 represents the extreme of incontrovertible evidence, while 0 represents the other extreme of utterly controvertible evidence. If the strength of my belief that I am typing right now is approximately 0.7, then the strength of evidence for my belief must be approximately 0.7 as well if it is to be sufficient.

Beyond the notion of sufficient evidence, notice that my understanding of having faith that God exists involves *recognizing* that one lacks sufficient evidence for one's belief that God exists. This is included for two reasons. First, and perhaps most importantly, cases involving this understanding of having faith that God exists are pervasive. As Hilary Kornblith writes,

> I've heard many people say quite sincerely, "I believe that God exists, but by my own lights, I am not justified in believing that God exists." . . . such a person believes that God exists, regards this belief as unjustified, and finds that so regarding the belief does not make it go out of existence.[1]

Similarly, T. J. Mawson writes,

> There are some who believe in God even though they do not take themselves to have any positive reasons for doing so and who do not consider themselves in any way intellectually irresponsible in so believing. Deciding whether or not there's a God, such people say, is a "leap of faith," rather than a conclusion of reason.[2]

Like Kornblith and Mawson, I too have encountered many theists—both personally and through various media—who have such faith that God exists. Pascal, Kierkegaard, and Bishop, for example, have this kind of faith that God exists. Indeed, the majority of the theists I have encountered have professed to having such faith that God exists, either straightaway or after some dialogue. (In cases of the latter, this is typically elicited as follows—the theist is asked on what grounds she believes that God exists, she lays out an argument for God's existence, objections are raised, and this is repeated for some time until the theist proclaims, "Well, all of this is beside the point, since I have faith that God exists.")

A second reason I include recognizing that one lacks sufficient evidence for believing that God exists in my understanding of having faith that God exists may be motivated by way of illustration. Suppose someone (Joe) believes that God exists and

---

[1] Hilary Kornblith (1986), "Naturalizing Rationality," In Newton Garver and Peter H. Hare (eds), *Naturalism and Rationality*. Buffalo, NY: Prometheus Books, 119.

[2] T. J. Mawson (2010), "The Ethics of Believing in God," *Think* 9(25): 93.

does so on the basis of what he deems to be sufficient evidence—a gut feeling. Suppose also that he is mistaken about having sufficient evidence for his belief—the strength of Joe's belief that God exists is 1, but the strength of his evidence for his belief—the gut feeling—is significantly less than 1. In this case, Joe believes that God exists, does so without having sufficient evidence for his belief, but does not recognize that he lacks sufficient evidence for this belief.

Now, some scholars seem to adopt an understanding of having faith such that, in this case, Joe has faith that God exists. That is, they seem to adopt an understanding of having faith such that believing that God exists without sufficient evidence is one and the same as having faith that God exists, *regardless* of whether one recognizes that one lacks sufficient evidence. Richard Dawkins, for example, understands faith to be "belief that isn't based on evidence."[3] And Richard Creel writes of "those who have faith that God exists, that is, those who have nonevidential confidence that God exists."[4] In neither of these understandings is the recognition that one lacks sufficient evidence stated explicitly to be a condition of having faith that God exists. (It may be that this condition is stated implicitly, of course; hence, my claim that they *seem* to adopt this understanding of faith.) But not including this condition—at least, not including it explicitly—strikes me as a seriously misleading omission. To be sure, *ex hypothesi*, Joe lacks sufficient evidence for his belief that God exists. But it seems misguided to say that he thereby has *faith* that God exists. Indeed, Joe himself would not profess to having faith that God exists; rather, he would profess to believing it on the basis of what he deems to be sufficient evidence—the gut feeling. There is reason to think, then, that having faith that God exists involves not only believing that God exists while lacking sufficient evidence for believing so, but also recognizing that one lacks sufficient evidence for believing so.

Possible misgivings

Of course, some philosophers and theologians have misgivings with such an under-standing of having faith. I will consider some of those misgivings here. Before doing so, however, it should be noted that the existence of such misgivings is unsurprising. For, as William Sessions writes, "Adequately characterizing faith is a much larger task than is commonly realized. In part this is because *the* concept of faith encompasses a variety of conceptions that differ in many ways."[5] Indeed, Robert Audi has identified

---

[3] Richard Dawkins (2008), "Science Versus Religion," In Louis P. Pojman and Michael Rea (eds), *Philosophy of Religion: An Anthology*, 5th edition. Belmont, CA: Thomson Wadsworth, 426. Also, Sam Harris, citing Paul Tillich, writes of faith as "an act of knowledge that has a low degree of evidence" (Sam Harris (2004), *The End of Faith*. New York, NY: W. W. Norton and Company, 65).

[4] Richard E. Creel (2003), "Faith as Imperfect Knowledge," In Elizabeth S. Radcliffe and Carol J. White (eds), *Faith in Theory and Practice: Essays on Justifying Religious Belief*. Peru, IL: Open Court Publishing, 69.

[5] William Sessions, "The Certainty of Faith," in *Faith in Theory and Practice*, 75. Paul Helm echoes Sessions' sentiments in this regard (see his *Belief Policies* (Cambridge: Cambridge University Press, 1994), Chapter 8).

seven different faith-locutions, including what he calls "propositional faith," "attitudinal faith," "creedal faith," "global faith," and "allegiant faith."[6]

As for particular misgivings, some philosophers claim that my understanding of having faith is not the "mainstream" understanding. Yet, the claims underpinning this misgiving are arguably false, at least in some cases. Consider, for example, comments I received from one philosopher in this regard:

> although many people understand . . . faith in this way, it is scarcely the mainstream understanding of . . . faith. I imagine that many Christians, for example, would say that they have faith that Christ died for our sins, and would say that an adequate reason for the truth of this proposition is that the Bible declares that it is true.[7]

Ironically, rather than justifying this philosopher's claim that my understanding of having faith is not mainstream, these comments support the view that it is. After all, what does it mean to say that many Christians have faith that Christ died for our sins *and* that they believe they have adequate reason to believe this? If such Christians really believe they have adequate reason to believe that Christ died for our sins, what are they adding—if anything at all—when they say that they have faith that Christ died for our sins? Faith has a nontrivial role to play in this claim, I submit, only if the reason they have for believing that Christ died for their sins is, by their own lights, somehow *in*adequate. So, if such Christians are representative of the mainstream view of having faith, as this philosopher suggests, then my understanding of having faith is indeed mainstream.

Second, some philosophers claim that my understanding of having faith does not accord with a particular philosopher's or theologian's understanding of having faith. There is no doubt that this is the case, at least with respect to some philosophers and theologians. Again, as Sessions contends, the concept of faith encompasses a variety of different conceptions. Even so, it is worth noting that this understanding of having faith is acknowledged, if not adopted, by many philosophers and theologians. For example, John Bishop writes that having faith that a proposition is true is "to take a proposition to be true in one's reasoning while recognizing that it is not the case that its truth is adequately supported by one's total available evidence."[8] Georges Rey writes that "many religious people readily recognize the failure of evidence but then go on to claim that religious beliefs are matters of 'faith,' not evidence . . ."[9] And, even Thomas Aquinas's understanding of having faith is seemingly identical to mine. According to Aquinas, there is

---

[6] Robert Audi (2008), "Belief, Faith, and Acceptance," *International Journal for Philosophy of Religion* 63: 92.

[7] Anonymous reviewer.

[8] John Bishop (2007), *Believing by Faith: An Essay in the Epistemology and Ethics of Religious Belief.* Oxford: Clarendon Press, 9.

[9] Georges Rey (2007), "Meta-Atheism: Religious Avowal as Self-Deception," In Louise M. Antony (ed.), *Philosophers without Gods: Meditations on Atheism and the Secular Life.* Oxford: Oxford University Press, 261.

a twofold mode of truth in what we profess about God. Some truths about God exceed all the ability of the human reason . . . But there are some truths which the natural reason also is able to reach . . . There are, consequently, some intelligible truths about God that are open to human reason; but there are others that absolutely surpass its power.[10]

However, due to various limitations—psychological, social, or other—most people are not able to obtain all the truths about God that are available through natural reason. Thus,

. . . it was necessary that the unshakeable certitude and pure truth concerning divine things should be presented to men by way of faith. Beneficially, therefore, did the divine Mercy provide that it should instruct us to hold by faith even those truths that the human reason is able to investigate.[11]

For Aquinas, then, we may come to believe things about God—including that he exists—with "unshakeable certitude," despite lacking sufficient evidence for these beliefs. Given this, one can see how Aquinas's understanding of having faith is seemingly identical to mine. For, according to Aquinas, in having faith that God exists, the strength of one's belief is 1, while the strength of one's evidence is (significantly) less than 1. And, importantly, those who have such faith recognize that they lack sufficient evidence. After all, they could not have such faith if they believed that they possessed sufficient evidence for their belief that God exists. All of this coincides with the understanding of having faith under consideration here—believing that God exists despite recognizing that one lacks sufficient evidence—evidence the strength of which is proportional to the strength of one's belief—for believing so.[12]

A final misgiving—some philosophers argue that understandings of having faith such as mine are defective since they involve *belief*, and having faith does not involve belief. In J. L. Schellenberg's words, having faith is "beliefless"—it involves "a purely voluntary attitude of mental assent toward that proposition, undertaken in circumstances where one views the state of affairs to which it refers as good and desirable but in which one lacks evidence causally sufficient for belief of the proposition."[13]

Having already agreed with Sessions that the concept of faith encompasses a variety of different conceptions, it should come as no surprise that I grant that this is one

---

[10] Thomas Aquinas (1996), "Faith, Analogy, and Five Proofs for God," In Ed. L. Miller (ed.), *Believing in God: Readings on Faith and Reason.* Upper Saddle River, NJ: Prentice Hall, 30–1.

[11] Ibid., 33.

[12] Both William Rowe and Paul Helm seem to understand Aquinas' view on having faith in this way as well. See William Rowe (2007), *Philosophy of Religion: An Introduction,* 4th edition. Belmont, CA: Wadsworth Publishing Company, 93; Paul Helm (1997), *Faith & Understanding.* Grand Rapids, MI: Wm. B. Eerdmans Publishing Co, 13.

[13] See J. L. Schellenberg (2005), *Prolegomena to a Philosophy of Religion.* Ithaca, NY: Cornell University Press, Chapters 5 and 6; and, J. L. Schellenberg (2007), *The Wisdom to Doubt: A Justification of Religious Skepticism.* Ithaca, NY: Cornell University Press, 7. For others who argue that faith that God exists does not involve belief, see Audi, "Belief, Faith, and Acceptance," 87–102; Brian Zamulinski, "Christianity and the Ethics of Belief," *Religious Studies* 44: 333–46.

conception of having faith. But even if I were to go further and grant that this is the *correct* conception of having faith, my moral argument against having faith that God exists would not be significantly affected. It's simply that, rather than being directed at *believing* that God exists, my argument would be directed at *voluntarily adopting an attitude of mental assent* toward the proposition "God exists."[14]

On the morality of having faith that God exists

With the preceding understanding of what it means to have faith that God exists in mind, we may now address the central question of this chapter—is it morally acceptable to have faith that God exists? That is, is it morally acceptable to believe that God exists despite recognizing that one lacks sufficient evidence for believing so? In what follows, I will be defending the following claim—in cases where believing that God exists will affect others, it is *prima facie* wrong to forgo attempting to proportion one's belief that God exists to the evidence. Lest there be any confusion, I will not be arguing that it is always wrong to have faith that God exists or even that it often is. I will simply be arguing that, under certain conditions, it can be. Hence the "*prima facie*" language—to say that it is *prima facie* wrong to forgo attempting to refrain from wronging others is to say that it is wrong *all else being equal*; it is not to say that it is *ultima facie* wrong, wrong *all things considered*.

My conclusion will no doubt strike some philosophers as rather conservative. Even so, I believe it reasonably splits the divide between two of the most popular positions on the morality of having faith that God exists—that of W. K. Clifford, on the one hand, who arguably overstates the moral obligation to believe that God exists on sufficient evidence, and that of the theists mentioned above, on the other, who find it perfectly acceptable to believe that God exists despite recognizing that they lack sufficient evidence for believing so.

Methodology: The commonsense approach

Before presenting my argument, a brief word about methodology is in order. For the purposes of this chapter, I adopt what I refer to as the "commonsense approach." The commonsense approach involves examining and evaluating the aforementioned question of faith in light of concepts and views constitutive of what is often referred

---

[14] One more possible misgiving about my understanding of having faith that God exists should be noted. Some philosophers—such as Jonathan Adler and Georges Rey—argue that believing something while recognizing that one lacks sufficient evidence for the belief is incoherent. As Rey writes, "try thinking something of the form: *p*, however I don't have adequate evidence or reasons for believing it . . . where you substitute for *p*, some non-religious claim, for example, '2 + 2 = 37,' 'the number of stars is even,' or 'Columbus sailed in 1962.' Imagine how baffling it would be if someone claimed merely to 'have faith' about these things" (Rey, "Meta-Atheism: Religious Avowal as Self-Deception," 260). See also Jonathan Adler (2006), *Belief's Own Ethics* Cambridge, MA: M.I.T. Press, 12ff. Not everyone agrees with Adler and Rey, of course: see Helm, *Belief Policies*, 193.

to as "commonsense morality." There are numerous ways in which one might attempt to characterize commonsense morality, such as by delineating what it considers to be morally relevant factors—factors that make morally right acts morally right and morally wrong acts morally wrong—and by delineating the moral claims typically associated it. For the purposes of this chapter, the latter will suffice.

As for the moral claims typically associated with commonsense morality, the one most pertinent to our discussion is shared by seemingly every moral theory, explicitly or implicitly—that it is *prima facie* wrong to forgo attempting to refrain from wronging others. It should be noted, moreover, that the claims commonsense morality makes are understood to be claims of moral *fact*. So, that it is *prima facie* wrong to forgo attempting to refrain from wronging others is a fact, according to common sense morality, just as it is a fact that $2 + 2 = 4$, that something is what it is, that some things were brought into existence, and so on.

With this said, a potential problem with my argument presents itself—it is only as good as the commonsense approach itself. I am happy to embrace this implication, if for no other reason than many of the theistic philosophers who think it is morally acceptable to have faith that God exists also embrace the commonsense approach. The following discussion, then, plays by such theistic philosophers' own rules, as it were.

The moral argument against faith

So, is it morally acceptable to have faith that God exists? Clifford, for one, emphatically denies that it is. "It is wrong always, everywhere and for anyone, to believe anything upon insufficient evidence," he writes.[15] But this is greatly overstated—surely it is not immoral for, say, an elderly woman on her deathbed privately to have faith that she is going to heaven. After all, her believing so does not endanger, harm, and/or violate the rights of anyone, nor does it make the world a worse place in any significant way. Of course, that Clifford has overstated the case does not entail that there are no conditions under which it is *prima facie* wrong to have faith that God exists. And, if my argument is sound—what I refer to as the "Moral Argument against Faith" (MAF)—then there are indeed conditions under which having faith that God exists is *prima facie* wrong. Stated formally, MAF is as follows:

> P1: In cases where one's doing something will affect others, it is *prima facie* wrong to forgo attempting to refrain from wronging those who will be affected by one's doing it.
>
> C1: In cases where believing that *p* will affect others, then, it is *prima facie* wrong to forgo attempting to refrain from wronging those who will be affected by one's so believing.
>
> P2: Attempting to refrain from wronging those who will be affected by one's believing that *p* involves attempting to believe that *p* on the basis of a doxastic practice that has proven itself to be nonarbitrarily reliable.

---

[15] W. K. Clifford, "The Ethics of Belief," in *Philosophy of Religion: An Anthology*, 367.

C2: In cases where believing that *p* will affect others, then, it is *prima facie* wrong to forgo attempting to believe that *p* on the basis of a doxastic practice that has proven itself to be nonarbitrarily reliable.

P3: The practice of proportioning one's beliefs to the evidence is the only doxastic practice that has proven itself to be nonarbitrarily reliable.

C3: In cases where believing that *p* will affect others, then, it is *prima facie* wrong to forgo attempting to proportion one's belief that *p* to the evidence.

As one can see, MAF may be used to argue that it is *prima facie* wrong to forgo attempting to proportion one's belief to the evidence for any given belief. For example, MAF may be used to argue that it is *prima facie* wrong for the aforementioned physician, mechanic, lawyer, et al. to forgo attempting to proportion their beliefs to the evidence. But, we are particularly concerned with belief that God exists. So, plugging in "God exists" for *p*, we get the following:

P1: In cases where one's doing something will affect others, it is *prima facie* wrong to forgo attempting to refrain from wronging those who will be affected by one's doing it.

C1: In cases where believing that God exists will affect others, then, it is *prima facie* wrong to forgo attempting to refrain from wronging those who will be affected by one's so believing.

P2: Attempting to refrain from wronging those who will be affected by one's believing that God exists involves attempting to believe that God exists on the basis of a doxastic practice that has proven itself to be nonarbitrarily reliable.

C2: In cases where believing that God exists will affect others, then, it is *prima facie* wrong to forgo attempting to believe that God exists on the basis of a doxastic practice that has proven itself to be nonarbitrarily reliable.

P3: The practice of proportioning one's beliefs to the evidence is the only doxastic practice that has proven itself to be nonarbitrarily reliable.

C3: In cases where believing that God exists will affect others, then, it is *prima facie* wrong to forgo attempting to proportion one's belief that God exists to the evidence.

In the following, I will defend each of the preceding premises in turn.

Defense of P1

As stated previously, not only is P1 constitutive of commonsense morality, it is shared by seemingly every moral theory. Rejecting P1, then, would be rather costly. It is hard to believe, then, that many theistic fideists would opt to reject it simply to make moral space for having faith as understood here, especially since one's having such faith may result in endangering, harming, and/or violating the rights of others. But, even if some theistic fideists were to reject P1, commonsense morality is constitutive of the methodology adopted for the purposes of this chapter, so I am assuming that P1 is true.

Defense of P2

My defense of P2 consists of two steps. The first step involves establishing how one comes to wrong another. There are numerous ways in which one may come to wrong another, of course, but the two ways most pertinent to this discussion are as follows: (1) by committing errors of moral fact, and (2) by committing errors of nonmoral fact. And, if it is not already obvious, it should be noted that these are doxastic errors—errors of belief about what are and are not moral and nonmoral facts.

Take, for example, murder. Insofar as there are moral facts—and there are, given commonsense morality—surely, one of them is that murder is morally wrong. And, when one wrongs another in this way, this may be the result of committing one or more of the following doxastic errors. First, it may be the result of erroneously believing that murder is not morally wrong or that the victim deserves to be killed. Either way, an error of moral fact is committed. Second, it may be the result of erroneously believing that one's victim is not genetically human or that one's victim has voluntarily consented to be killed. Either way, an error of nonmoral fact is committed. Attempting to refrain from wronging those who will be affected by one's believing something, then, involves attempting to refrain from committing errors of moral and nonmoral fact, among other things.

This brings us to the second step. Given that wronging others may be the result of committing errors of moral and nonmoral fact, attempting to refrain from wronging others involves attempting to refrain from committing such errors. But what does attempting to refrain from committing such errors involve? If it is to be a sincere (dare I say, good faith) attempt, it involves attempting to believe purported statements of moral and nonmoral fact on the basis of a fact-determining doxastic practice that has proven itself to be nonarbitrarily reliable. Perhaps the clearest way to convey what I mean by a "fact-determining doxastic practice that has proven itself to be nonarbitrarily reliable" is to break this clause into its constitutive parts and analyze them in piecemeal fashion. Thus:

- By a "doxastic practice," I mean a belief-generating practice.
- By a "fact-determining" doxastic practice, I mean a doxastic practice that pertains to facts as opposed to mere opinions or tastes. The reason for this should be obvious—the issue at hand is what attempting to refrain from committing errors of moral and nonmoral *fact* involves. Thus, whatever doxastic practice is proposed as a solution, it should be one that pertains to facts, not mere opinions or tastes.

And,

- By a doxastic practice that has "proven itself to be nonarbitrarily reliable," I mean a doxastic practice that (a) generally can be counted on to generate true or probably true beliefs and (b) can do so such that there is an appropriate causal relation between the belief and the doxastic practice itself. It is important that the doxastic practice be reliable since one is attempting to acquire true—not merely justified—beliefs about purported statements of moral and nonmoral fact. And it is important that the doxastic practice be nonarbitrarily reliable so as to rule out doxastic practices that may be reliable, but nevertheless should be rejected. Consider, for example, the doxastic practice of flipping a coin in order to decide whether or not to believe any given statement.[16] Such a practice *might* turn out to be reliable in that it *might* generally be counted on to generate true or probably true beliefs. But, even if it did, we ought to reject it and do so on the grounds that there is not an appropriate causal relation between the true or probably true beliefs and the doxastic practice itself.

That attempting to refrain from committing errors of moral and nonmoral fact involves attempting to believe purported statements of moral and nonmoral fact on the basis of such a doxastic may be seen as follows.

Consider cases of punishment, legal or other. Whether or not to punish someone for something he allegedly did—say, stealing a diamond bracelet—is a moral matter, at least in part. How, in good faith, would we attempt to refrain from wrongly punishing such an individual? We would attempt to refrain from committing errors of moral and nonmoral fact, among other things. And we would do this by believing the relevant moral facts (that something was (or was not) done that is deserving of punishment— whatever the moral facts may be) and nonmoral facts (that the accused did (or did not) steal the bracelet, that the alleged diamond bracelet *really is* a diamond bracelet— whatever the nonmoral facts may be) on the basis of a fact-determining doxastic practice that has proven itself to be nonarbitrarily reliable. We would not attempt to refrain from committing errors of moral and nonmoral fact on the basis of a doxastic practice that cannot be generally counted on to generate true or probably true beliefs (such as reading tea leaves) or on the basis of a doxastic practice that lacks an appropriate causal relation between the true or probably true beliefs and the doxastic practice itself (such as flipping a coin). To do either of these things would be unacceptable—morally, if not otherwise.

Or, to take a case not involving punishment, suppose a new, seemingly sentient and sapient life form—one uncannily reminiscent of E. T. from Steven Spielberg's *E.T.: The Extra-Terrestrial*—were discovered on Earth and we were genuinely concerned about not wronging it by, say, killing it. How, in good faith, would we attempt to refrain from doing so? Again, we would attempt to refrain from committing errors of moral and nonmoral fact. And we would do this by believing the relevant moral facts (that killing this life form is morally wrong, or morally acceptable, or morally required— whatever the moral facts may be) and nonmoral facts (that this new life form is indeed sentient and sapient, or not sentient, or not sapient—whatever the nonmoral facts may be) on the basis of a fact-determining doxastic practice that has proven itself to be nonarbitrarily reliable. We would not attempt to refrain from committing errors of

---

[16] The possibility of such a doxastic practice is discussed in George Mavrodes's (1983), "Jerusalem and Athens Revisited," in *Faith and Rationality: Reason and Belief in God.* Notre Dame, IN: University of Notre Dame Press, 209.

moral and nonmoral fact by reading tea leaves or flipping a coin. To do either of these things would be unacceptable—morally, if not otherwise.

Attempting to refrain from committing errors of moral and nonmoral fact, then, involves attempting to believe purported statements of moral and nonmoral fact on the basis of a doxastic practice that has proven itself to be nonarbitrarily reliable.

Defense of P3

This brings us to the third and final premise. The only fact-determining doxastic practice that has proven itself to be nonarbitrarily reliable is proportioning one's beliefs to the evidence. The case for this is overwhelming and can be stated quite succinctly.

Consider, for example, the history of intellectual progress. Specifically, consider not only how far we have come in the natural sciences, the social sciences, the humanities, etc., but the doxastic practice through which we have come this far. The progress in each of these fields is both undeniable and impressive. And, the doxastic practice through which we have come this far—particularly in more recent history—is principally that of proportioning beliefs to the evidence. This is not to say that, as a species, we have *always* proportioned our beliefs to the evidence, or that all intellectual progress is rooted in doing so. It is simply to say that, when we reflect upon the history of intellectual progress, we see a stronger and stronger correlation between proportioning beliefs to the evidence and intellectual progress. As a result, we have come to deem this doxastic practice to be one that has proven itself to be reliable in this domain. (There is no better place to witness that we deem this doxastic practice to be one that has proven itself reliable in this domain than the place wherein intellectual development is expected to occur—the classroom.) No other fact-determining doxastic practice can claim a comparable history of success. Indeed, it is difficult to think of a non-evidence-based, fact-determining doxastic practice that is a potential contender. A thorough presentation of this fact would involve describing in great detail the history of each of these fields, but for the sake of avoiding too great a digression, I will trust you are sufficiently familiar with their histories to grant the point.[17]

Consider, also, the history of moral progress. There is no doubt that moral progress—particularly when understood in terms of commonsense morality—has occurred throughout history. What was once considered morally acceptable in many societies—such as slavery, torture, the eye-for-an-eye principle of justice (at least, the literal implementation of it), the unequal treatment of women and racial minorities, etc.—is now largely condemned as immoral. And, the doxastic practice through which we have progressed so—particularly in more recent history—is principally that of proportioning beliefs to the evidence. Again, this is not to say that, as a species, we have always proportioned our beliefs to the evidence, or that all moral progress is rooted in doing so. It is simply to say that, when we reflect upon the history of moral progress, we

---

[17] If you are not sufficiently familiar with the history of these progresses, a perusal of the relevant entries in an encyclopedia is a good place to start.

see a stronger and stronger correlation between proportioning beliefs to the evidence and moral progress. As a result, we have come to deem this doxastic practice to be one that has proven itself to be reliable in this domain. (There is no better place to witness that we deem this doxastic practice as one that has proven itself reliable in this domain than in a college course on ethics.) As with the history of intellectual progress, a thorough presentation of the history of moral progress would involve describing in great detail the history of moral progress. But, again, for the sake of avoiding too great a digression, I will trust you are sufficiently familiar with their histories to grant the point.[18]

And, lest there be any doubt, this doxastic practice is nonarbitrarily reliable—there is indeed an appropriate causal relation between true or probably true beliefs and the doxastic practice of proportioning one's beliefs to the evidence. Though a thorough defense of this claim requires more space than is available here, it is worth briefly covering one of the foremost defenses of it, provided by Jonathan Adler.[19]

Adler defends what he calls the "subjective principle of sufficient reason," which is as follows—when one attends *in full awareness* to any of one's beliefs, one must regard it as believed for sufficient or adequate reasons, by which Adler means evidence the strength of which is proportional to the strength of one's belief.[20] (I emphasize "in full awareness" in order to make clear that this principle is consistent with my claim that people have faith that God exists as understood here—such individuals presumably do not attend to their belief that God exists in full awareness.) His reasons for thinking this principle is true are twofold. First, we find ourselves compelled to *follow* this principle. As he writes,

> The compulsion is due to our recognition, when attending to any particular belief, that we are entitled to the belief only if it is well founded. That we do follow it is then a reflection of our grasping the demands of belief, not merely a curious psychological truth about us.[21]

Second, we find ourselves compelled to *attribute* the principle to others, at least for what they *assert*. But, as he writes, "The requirement that assertions be backed by good reasons, since they claim the truth of what is asserted, is just the analogue of the requirement that beliefs be backed by good reasons, since upon awareness they claim the truth of what is believed."[22] And, it is *belief itself* which demands that we possess sufficient evidence for our beliefs. He writes,

---

[18] Again, if you are not sufficiently familiar with the history of these progresses, a perusal of the relevant entries in an encyclopedia is a good place to start. See also Lawrence C. Becker and Charlotte B. Becker (eds) (2003), *A History of Western Ethics*, 2nd edition. New York, NY: Routledge; Alasdair MacIntyre (1998), *A Short History of Ethics: A History of Moral Philosophy from the Homeric Age to the Twentieth Century*. New York, NY: Routledge.

[19] See Adler's *Belief's Own Ethics*.

[20] Ibid., 26, emphasis mine.

[21] Ibid., 27.

[22] Ibid., 27.

Since one's beliefs are what one regards as true when we attend to any of our beliefs, a claim is made on us for holding that the belief is true. So it is belief that requires proportional reasons or evidence, not any external source.[23]

Each of these things—that we find ourselves compelled to follow the subjective principle of sufficient reason, that we attribute the subjective principle of sufficient reason to others, and that it is belief itself that demands that we possess sufficient evidence for our beliefs—indicates that there is indeed an appropriate causal relation between true or probably true beliefs and the doxastic practice of proportioning one's beliefs to the evidence.

All of this supports the view that proportioning one's beliefs to the evidence is the only fact-determining doxastic practice that has proven itself to be nonarbitrarily reliable. This is not to say, of course, that proportioning one's beliefs to the evidence always generates true or probably true beliefs, only that it reliably does, as the trajectories of intellectual and moral development reveal. And, clearly, it remains possible that there is another fact-determining doxastic practice that may be capable of proving itself to be nonarbitrarily reliable. But, if there is, it is one of which we are currently unaware. At least for now, then, a good faith attempt to refrain from committing errors of moral and nonmoral fact and, in turn, wronging others involves attempting to proportion one's beliefs to the evidence.

Summary

My moral argument against having faith that God exists (MAF) may be summarized as follows. In cases where one's doing something will affect others, it is *prima facie* wrong to forgo attempting to refrain from wronging those who will be affected by one's doing it. In cases where believing that God exists will affect others, then, it is *prima facie* wrong to forgo attempting to refrain from wronging those who will be affected by one's so believing. Attempting to refrain from wronging those who will be affected by one's believing that God exists involves attempting to refrain from committing errors of moral and nonmoral fact. And this involves attempting to believe purported statements of moral and nonmoral fact—including the nonmoral statement "God exists"—on the basis of a fact-determining doxastic practice that has proven itself to be nonarbitrarily reliable. The only fact-determining doxastic practice that has proven itself to be nonarbitrarily reliable is proportioning one's beliefs to the evidence. Thus, attempting to refrain from wronging those who will be affected by one's believing that God exists involves attempting to proportion one's belief that God exists to the evidence. In cases where believing that God exists will affect others, then, it is *prima facie* wrong to forgo attempting to proportion one's belief that God exists to the evidence.

---

[23] Ibid., 5.

A caveat

At this point, an important caveat is in order. The extent to which believing something will affect others is a function of the content of the belief itself, among other things. For, content-wise, some beliefs are more others-regarding than others. The belief that people are never to be trusted, for example, is more others-regarding than the belief that unicorns have four legs, since the former makes a claim about how one is to behave with respect to others while the latter does not. Given this, one might maintain that the extent to which it is *prima facie* wrong to forgo attempting to proportion one's beliefs to the evidence is proportional to the extent to which the belief is others-regarding—the more others-regarding the belief, the worse it is to forgo attempting to proportion one's beliefs to the evidence, all else being equal. Though Clifford (for one) would likely reject this, I will grant that this is the case.[24]

The extent to which it is *prima facie* wrong to forgo attempting to proportion one's belief that God exists to the evidence, then, depends on the extent to which the belief that God exists is others-regarding. The question is—to what extent is the belief that God exists others-regarding? Some might think that it is not others-regarding at all, while others might think that it is others-regarding to one extent or another. Rather than settling this dispute, I will simply submit the following.

First, if the belief that God exists, in and of itself, is not others-regarding, then the extent to which it is *prima facie* wrong to forgo attempting to proportion one's belief that God exists to the evidence is zero. Even if this is the case, however, it does not follow that having faith that God exists is never *prima facie* wrong. This would be true only if having faith that God exists were done in a vacuum, independent of other beliefs. But such is generally not the case. Specifically, theistic philosophers and other theists tend to believe not simply that God exists, but that God would have us behave in various ways, including ways which are others-regarding. So, even if the belief that God exists, in and of itself, is not directly others-regarding, it tends to be conjoined with others-regarding beliefs in such a way that it becomes indirectly others-regarding. This brings us to the second possibility.

If the belief that God exists, in and of itself, is not others-regarding, but *is* others-regarding when combined with other beliefs, then the extent to which it is *prima facie* wrong to forgo attempting to proportion these beliefs to the evidence is proportional to the extent to which the conjunction of these beliefs is others-regarding. Take, for example, the beliefs that God exists and that he wants wives to submit to their husbands. The extent to which it is *prima facie* wrong to forgo attempting to proportion these beliefs to the evidence will be proportional to the extent to which the conjunction of these beliefs—that God exists and that God wants wives to submit to their husbands— is others-regarding.

---

[24] Clifford held that even believing statements that are not others-regarding on the basis of insufficient evidence has deleterious effects, such as making the individual who does so (repeatedly) more gullible and, in turn, more susceptible to believing on the basis of insufficient evidence statements that *are* others-regarding.

Finally, if the belief that God exists, in and of itself, is others-regarding, then the extent to which it is *prima facie* wrong to forgo attempting to proportion the belief that God exists to the evidence is proportional to the extent to which the belief that God exists is others-regarding.

Applying MAF to other religious beliefs

Before moving on to possible objections, I would like to motivate MAF further by applying it to various religions and, in particular, some of their respective constitutive beliefs. Take Raëlism, the religion that teaches that life on Earth was scientifically created by a species of intelligent extraterrestrials. Among other things, Raëlians believe that in order to usher in the "Great Return"—the return of our alleged extraterrestrial creators—an embassy must be built, preferably in Jerusalem.[25] Accordingly, they believe that such an embassy *ought* to be built. Now, the belief "An embassy for our extraterrestrial creators ought to be built, preferably in Jerusalem" is clearly others-regarding. Given this, and given MAF, it is *prima facie* wrong to forgo attempting to proportion this belief to the evidence. And this seems to be the correct verdict.

Or, take the Church of Satan, a religion which emphasizes the use of reason, among other things (but not, despite their name, the worship of Satan). The Church of Satan has what they refer to as "Eleven Satanic Rules of the Earth," one of which is—"When walking in open territory, bother no one. If someone bothers you, ask them to stop. If they don't stop, destroy them."[26] Now, the belief "I ought to destroy he who does not stop bothering me after I've asked him to" is clearly others-regarding. Given this, and given MAF, it is *prima facie* wrong to forgo attempting to proportion this belief to the evidence. And, once again, this seems to be the correct verdict.

Or, finally, consider the Church of Jesus Christ of the Latter-Day Saints (LDS). According to LDS's "law of chastity," only sexual activity between a man and his wife is morally permissible—any other sexual activity is immoral. Homosexual activity, then, is proscribed by the law of chastity—"Those who find themselves struggling with sexual temptations, including feelings of same-gender attraction, should not give in to those temptations."[27] Moreover, LDS holds (at least, once held) that this should be reflected in the law; hence its significant financial support of Proposition 8, a constitutional amendment that banned same-sex marriage in California. Now, the beliefs "One should not give into feelings of same-gender attraction" and "We ought to support the ban on same-sex marriage in California" are clearly others-regarding. Given this, and given MAF, it is *prima facie* wrong to forgo attempting to proportion these beliefs to the evidence. Once again, this seems to be the correct verdict.

---

[25] http://www.elohimembassy.org./why-an-embassy.php.
[26] http://www.churchofsatan.com/home.html.
[27] http://www.lds.org/ldsorg/v/index.jsp?locale=0&sourceId=23e80bbce1d98010VgnVCM1000004d 82620a____&vgnextoid=bbd508f54922d010VgnVCM1000004d82620aRCRD.

Objections

There are numerous objections that may be raised against MAF; indeed, too many to be addressed here. For the sake of space, I will limit myself to four.

Doesn't MAF prove too much?

Some might contend that MAF proves too much. Consider, for example, the following statements:

- Ducks exist independently of us.
- Other people are not actually robots.
- One's memories tend to be reliable.

Surely, some might argue, it is not *prima facie* wrong to forgo attempting to proportion belief in these things to the evidence.

But, of course, if MAF is sound, then it *is prima facie* wrong to forgo attempting to proportion belief in these things to the evidence, and more than mere declaration is needed here. Each of these statements is others-regarding, after all, either in and of itself, or when combined with other beliefs. Accordingly, if one is to attempt to refrain from wronging those who will be affected by one's believing them, one ought to attempt to proportion one's beliefs to the evidence. To forgo doing so would be *prima facie* wrong.

Moreover, this objection takes too much for granted, as it assumes that believing these things cannot ever be morally problematic. But, of course, it can be, depending on the context in which these things are believed. For example, if the context in which one believes that one's memories tend to be reliable is such that another will be harmed by one's so believing, then it can be morally problematic for one to believe that one's memories tend to be reliable. If one is to attempt to refrain from wronging those who will be affected by one's so believing, then, one ought to attempt to proportion one's belief to the evidence.

That said, and perhaps more to the point, to be *prima facie* wrong to forgo attempting to proportion one's belief to the evidence is to be wrong, *all else being equal*. This is consistent with the claim that it is *not* wrong to forgo attempting to proportion one's belief to the evidence, all things considered. In this case, one can consistently hold that, though it is wrong for one to forgo attempting to proportion one's belief in these things to the evidence, all else being equal, it may *not* be wrong for one to forgo attempting to proportion one's belief in these things to the evidence, all things considered. And this strikes me as the correct verdict.

Consider, next, the following statements:

- My son will beat cancer.
- My daughter will be successful.
- My future will be better than my past.

Once again, some might argue that it is not *prima facie* wrong to forgo attempting to proportion belief in these things to the evidence. But, there are at least two reasons to think this objection is misguided.

First, in many cases, statements such as these are properly understood to be statements of hope or desire rather than statements of belief. Accordingly, they are not instances of forgoing attempting to proportion belief to the evidence.

Second, even in cases where statements such as these are not statements of hope or desire, but instead, statements of belief, such statements fail to serve as counterexamples to MAF's conclusion. To see this, consider the case of Madeline Neumann, an 11-year-old girl who died after her parents prayed for healing rather than seek medical help for a treatable form of diabetes. According to the local police chief, the girl's parents attributed the death to not having "enough faith."[28] Now, whether the Neumanns understand "having faith" as it is understood here is unclear, but it need not be clear to make my point, which is—*if* the Neumann's believed that their daughter would survive without medical treatment while recognizing that they lacked sufficient evidence for believing so, and *if* they did not attempt to proportion their belief to the evidence, then, according to MAF, their having such faith was *prima facie* wrong. And this seems to be the correct verdict.[29]

Or, finally, consider the following statements:

- God wants me to love others.
- God wants me to help those in need.
- God wants me to be good to others.

Once again, some might argue that it is not *prima facie* wrong to forgo attempting to proportion belief in these things to the evidence. After all, loving others, helping those who are in need, and being good to others are morally commendable acts.[30]

But, again, if MAF is correct, then it is *prima facie* wrong to forgo attempting to proportion belief in these things to the evidence, and more than mere declaration is needed here. Moreover, this objection also takes too much for granted, as it assumes that doing what God wants—even loving others, helping those in need, being good to others—cannot be morally problematic. But, of course, it can be morally problematic—depending on one's understanding of God and, specifically, his desires and commands, "loving," "helping," and "being good to" others may involve doing what many people would deem, in fact, to be bad. During the various inquisitions, for example, "helping" others turn from their heretical ways involved torturing and even killing them, among other things. More recently, "loving,"

---

[28] http://www.foxnews.com/story/0,2933,341574,00.html.
[29] Incidentally, this seems to be reflected in the legal outcome of this case. Though there is not a one-to-one correspondence between the moral and legal status of acts, it is worth noting that the mother was subsequently convicted of second-degree *reckless* homicide. See http://scienceblogs.com/insolence/2009/05/guilty_guilty_guilty_the_mother_who_reli.php.
[30] Thanks to John Lemos for raising this issue.

"helping," and "being good to" others has involved picketing the funerals of dead soldiers, informing those mourning that "God hates fags" (à la the Westboro Baptist Church), relying solely on prayer for healing rather than seeking medical help for treatable life-threatening illnesses (à la the Neumanns), crucifying and ultimately killing a nun during a would-be exorcism (à la a Romanian priest along with four other nuns), and so on.[31]

Finally, as with a previous reply, to be *prima facie* wrong to forgo attempting to proportion one's belief in these things to the evidence is to be wrong, all else being equal. In this case, one can consistently hold that, though it is wrong to forgo attempting to proportion one's belief in these things to the evidence, all else being equal, it may *not* be wrong to forgo attempting to proportion one's belief in these things to the evidence, all things considered. And this strikes me as the correct verdict.

Are we responsible for what we believe?

Another objection to MAF may be elicited by asking the following questions. First, doesn't MAF entail that we can control what we believe and, thus, that we are responsible for what we believe? If so, doesn't this render MAF defective, since we are not in control of what we believe?

Before addressing the issue of whether we can control and are responsible for what we believe, it should be noted that we certainly behave as if we can and are (respectively) —we regularly blame people for believing things we think they ought not to believe ("He should've known better"), and we regularly praise people who believe things we think they ought to believe. Indeed, some theists—particularly fundamentalists—are paragons of such behavior—in no uncertain terms, they blame atheists and agnostics for their unbelief and praise those who forgo their unbelief for belief (or, at least, they inform atheists and agnostics that *God* blames them for their unbelief and will reward them for forgoing unbelief for belief). Granted, that we behave this way does not entail that, as a matter of fact, we *can* control and are responsible for what we believe. But that we behave this way is a relevant consideration in determining whether we are so in control and responsible.

That said, regarding the first question—whether MAF entails that we can control and are responsible for what we believe—simply put, it does not entail this. Nor, however, does it entail that we cannot control and are not responsible for what we believe. Strictly speaking, MAF entails the following—*to the extent* that we can control and are responsible for what we believe, it is *prima facie* wrong to forgo attempting to proportion one's beliefs to the evidence when one's believing will affect others. This is perfectly consistent both with the view that we can control and are responsible for

---

[31] For the Westboro Baptist Church, see http://www.godhatesfags.com/; for the crucifixion of the nun, http://news.bbc.co.uk/2/hi/europe/4107524.stm.

what we believe as well as the view that we cannot control and are not responsible for what we believe. MAF does not entail, then, that we can control and are responsible for what we believe.

But even if it did—and in answer to the second question—this would not render MAF defective. For, though we may not have direct control over what we believe—though we may not be able to *will* ourselves to adopt any given belief—we nevertheless have indirect control over what we believe. Indeed, both atheistic and theistic philosophers agree that we have indirect control over what we believe. As the atheistic philosopher Adler writes,

> for many of our beliefs we do have the ability to influence and shape the dispositions underlying their acceptance. If you are quick to ascribe ill motives to others, you have probably had many occasions to discern and evaluate this pattern of your attributions and you can undertake to control them accordingly. The modification does not require direct control over your believing.[32]

And the theistic philosopher Alston writes:

> . . . I do have voluntary control over moves that can influence a particular belief formation—for example, looking for more evidence or selectively exposing myself to evidence—and moves that can affect my general belief-forming habits or tendencies—for example, training myself to be more critical of testimony.[33]

If Adler and Alston are correct about this—and it seems to me that they are—then we can control what we believe, at least indirectly. Granted, from the mere fact that Adler and Alston believe that we can control what we believe indirectly, it does not immediately follow that we actually can. In the spirit of this chapter, then, we would want to know what evidence they have for this. For the sake of space, I will forgo this discussion and refer you to the relevant literature.[34]

Of course, even if this is correct, it does not follow that we have the ability to influence and shape the dispositions underlying the acceptance of *all* of our beliefs. To use examples from above, it may be that we do not have the ability to influence and shape the dispositions underlying the acceptance of the beliefs that ducks exist independently of us, that other people are not actually robots, or that one's memories tend to be reliable. Try as we might, we may not be able to reject

---

[32] Adler, 66.

[33] William P. Alston, "Christian Experience and Christian Belief," in *Faith and Rationality: Reason and Belief in God*, 114. See also Richard Swinburne (1981), *Faith and Reason*. Oxford: Clarendon Press, 26.

[34] See Adler, 66ff; Alston, 114ff. It should be noted here that some philosophers have argued for the stronger view that we have direct control over some of our beliefs. See Ronney Mourad (2008), "Choosing to Believe," *International Journal for Philosophy of Religion* 63: 55–69; Paul Helm, *Belief Policies*, Chapter 2.

these beliefs; at least, we may not be able to reject these beliefs while remaining sane.[35]

But even if we do not have the ability to influence and shape the dispositions underlying the acceptance of all of our beliefs, it does not follow that we do not have the ability to influence and shape the disposition underlying the acceptance of a *particular* belief—that an invisible, omniscient, omnipotent, perfectly good being exists. Belief in the existence of God is significantly different from belief that ducks exist independent of us, that other people are not actually robots, and that one's memories tend to be reliable. We may not be able to reject the latter beliefs, but we *are* able to reject the former belief. Indeed, if religious affiliation is any indication, more than half the world's population does just this—according to Oxford University Press's *World Christian Encyclopedia*, in 2009, only a little over 3 billion out of the world's 6.8 billion were adherents of religions that include belief in God as understood here.[36] Moreover, since being an adherent of a religion does not entail that one *really* believes that God exists, the number of believers in God's existence is likely to be (much) smaller.[37] So, even if we do not have the ability to influence and shape the dispositions underlying the acceptance of all of our beliefs, it does not follow that we do not have the ability to influence and shape the disposition underlying the acceptance of the belief that God exists.

---

[35] An anonymous reviewer took issue with my claim that we may not be able to help believing that, say, physical objects exist, noting, "For one thing, Pyrrhonist skeptics have claimed to have a fair degree of success in carrying out a policy of withholding belief while, with respect to their attitudes and actions, being guided by appearances." Now, I am no expert on Pyrrhonist skepticism, and I have no doubt that the reviewer is correct in saying that they *claimed* to have had such success. But, I find it nearly impossible to believe that being guided by beliefs regarding mere appearances rather than being guided by beliefs regarding the real existence of physical objects—including not only ducks, but stampeding horses, swinging swords, incoming spears, falling rocks, food, doors, etc.—is conducive for successfully navigating through life. After all, mere appearances are just that, *mere* appearances. So, unless one *also* thinks that appearances give us good reason to believe that physical objects really exist, I fail to see how mere appearances could serve one in successfully navigating through life. "I am being appeared to sword-swingingly; thus, I ought to move out of the way" makes sense if the *appearance* of a swinging sword gives one good reason to believe that the swinging sword *really exists*. And if it does give one good reason to think that the swinging sword really exists, then it is doubtful that Pyrrhonist skeptics *really* withheld belief about the real existence of physical objects. On the other hand, if being appeared to sword-swingingly does *not* give one good reason to believe that a swinging sword really exists, then what possible role could such appearances play in one's successful navigation of life? In other words, if mere appearances do not give one good reason to believe that a physical objects really exists, how are they any better at helping us successfully navigate through life than fictions or fantasies? All this to say, I rather doubt Pyrrhonist skeptics *really* suspended judgments about physical objects. Moreover, Pyrrhonist skepticism notwithstanding, the claim that we may not be able to reject these beliefs remains true for those of us who are not Pyrrhonist skeptics.

[36] D. B. Barrett, G. T. Kurian, and T. M. Johnson (eds) (2001), *World Christian Encyclopedia: A Comparative Survey of Churches and Religions in the Modern World*, 2 vols. New York, NY: Oxford University Press.

[37] Daniel Dennett's "belief in belief" is pertinent here. See Daniel Dennett (2006), *Breaking the Spell: Religion as a Natural Phenomenon*. New York, NY: Viking Adult, Chapter 8.

Isn't MAF question-begging?

One might object that MAF begs the question against theistic fideists and anyone else who may think it is morally acceptable to have faith that God exists. Specifically, one might argue as follows:

> *The issue at hand is whether it is morally acceptable to have faith that God exists. You have argued that, when believing that God exists will affect others, it is prima facie wrong to forgo attempting to proportion one's belief to the evidence. And you have done so by providing what you deem to be sufficient evidence, namely, MAF. You have thereby assumed that the issue of whether it is morally acceptable to have faith that God exists is to be settled on evidential grounds. But, in so doing, you have begged the question against those who hold that having faith that God exists is morally acceptable.*

This objection is misguided as it erroneously conflates two distinct questions. One question pertains to whether it is morally acceptable to have faith that God exists. A second question pertains to how we should go about answering that first question—the question of whether it is morally acceptable to have faith that God exists. According to this objection, if the answer to the second question is, "We should go about answering the first question on evidential grounds," then the answer to the first question must be "It is not morally acceptable to believe that God exists while recognizing that one lacks sufficient evidence—to have faith that God exists—at least in some cases." But this does not follow. Even if the answer to the second question is, "We should go about answering the first question on evidential grounds," it is logically possible for the answer to the first question to be "It is morally acceptable to believe that God exists while recognizing that one lacks sufficient evidence."

Accordingly, even though my answer to the second question is "We should go about answering the first question on evidential grounds" (as is indicated by my use of MAF), it does not immediately follow that it is not morally acceptable to believe that God exists while recognizing that one lacks sufficient evidence—to have faith that God exists. Thus, it is not the case that MAF begs the question against theistic fideists or anyone else who may think it is morally acceptable to have faith that God exists.

Isn't it prudent to have faith that God exists?

A fourth and final objection to MAF is as follows—given the benefits of people having faith that God exists—such as the good works done in God's name, the sense of meaning and hope it gives them, the possibility of eternal bliss (à la Pascal), the possibility of not having every moment wasted (à la Kierkegaard), etc.—isn't it prudent for people to have such faith?

To be sure, there are benefits of people having faith that God exists, at least in some cases. But, it does not follow from this that there aren't also problems with their doing so. To begin with, from the fact that doing something is beneficial, it does not follow that it is thereby morally acceptable. Under certain conditions, it may be beneficial to cheat, lie, or steal, for example, but it does not follow from this that cheating, lying, or stealing in such circumstances is not *prima facie* wrong.

Second, there are disadvantages of people having faith that God exists. Violence and other deplorable acts committed in the name of God have a long and shameful history. And we would be fooling ourselves if we thought that none of it was causally linked with having faith that God exists. To be sure, whether any particular instance of these things is causally linked with having faith that God exists might be difficult to establish, but it stands to reason that at least some of them are.

Indeed, speaking of prudence, it would be prudent not to be too skeptical of the preceding claim. For if one thinks that we cannot know that violence done in God's name is causally linked with the perpetrators' having faith that God exists, then, by parity of reasoning, one should also think that we cannot know that good works done in God's name are causally linked with the do-gooders' having faith that God exists. After all, the alleged epistemic gap there is between us and those who commit bad works in God's name does not disappear simply by substituting individuals who commit good works in God's name. For the epistemic gap pertains to the beliefs underlying the actions, not the actions themselves. Whether the works done in God's name are good or bad, then, is irrelevant to whether there is indeed such an epistemic gap. All this to say, if we cannot know that some instances of bad works are causally linked with people having faith that God exists, then we cannot know that some instances of good works are causally linked with people having faith that God exists. And if this is the case, then the objection under consideration—that it is beneficial for people to have faith that God exists—is undermined.

Finally, as discussed above, there are benefits of people proportioning their beliefs to the evidence. Indeed, if what I argued above is correct, both intellectual and moral progress is explained principally in terms of people proportioning their beliefs to the evidence.[38]

(Regarding Pascal's and Kierkegaard's beneficial reasons for having faith that God exists, the criticisms are well documented and need not be repeated here. I refer you, then, to the relevant literature.[39])

---

[38] A point similar to one made in the introductory chapter is worth emphasizing here—from the fact that there are benefits of people having faith that God exists (or anything else, for that matter), it does not follow that that which is believed on the basis of faith is true. In short, beneficial beliefs do not as such confer truth on that which is believed. Both the Christian who has faith that Jesus is God and the Muslim who has faith that Allah—not Jesus—is God perform good works in God's name. But, one of them has a false belief; their respective beliefs about who God is cannot both be correct. Unfortunately, this lesson is lost on many people; I have encountered many theists who erroneously draw inferences regarding the truth of their theistic beliefs from the good works performed in the name of God.

[39] See, for example, Simon Blackburn, "Pascal's Wager: A Critique," in *Exploring Philosophy of Religion: An Introductory Anthology*, 193–95; and, Michael Peterson, et al. (2009), *Reason & Religious Belief: An Introduction to the Philosophy of Religion*, 4th edition. New York, NY: Oxford University Press, 59ff.

Conclusion

Unlike theistic inferentialists and theistic noninferentialists, theistic fideists believe that there is no discoverable probabilifying evidence of God's existence. Even so, they hold that it is acceptable—morally, if not otherwise—to have faith that God exists. If the argument I have presented here (MAF) is sound, there is at least one condition under which it is *prima facie* wrong to have faith that God exists—when one's belief that God exists will affect others and one has not attempted to believe that God exists on the basis of sufficient evidence.[40]

---

[40] Though my argument has focused on the possibility of wronging *others*, Allen Wood has argued that having faith can be wrong on *self-regarding* grounds. See Allen Wood (2008), "The Duty to Believe According to the Evidence," *International Journal for Philosophy of Religion* 63: 7–24.

5

A Problem for All Three
Theistic Philosophers

Introduction

I have argued thus far that each of the three types of theistic philosopher under consideration faces a problem unique to his or her type. The problem theistic inferentialists face—the problem of the theistic inferentialists—is that they have failed to make the inferential evidential case for theism to their skeptical counterparts. The problem theistic noninferentialists face—the problem of the hiddenness of God—is that the noninferential evidence of God's existence that allegedly exists is scarcely apprehended, if it is apprehended at all. And, the problem theistic fideists face—the problem of faith—is that there is at least one condition under which having faith that God exists is *prima facie* wrong.

In addition to the particular problems each type of theistic philosopher faces, there are two problems that all three types of theistic philosopher share, one of which will be discussed in this chapter, the other of which will be discussed in the next chapter.

The problem of skeptical theism

All three types of theistic philosopher assume that we can know what God would do (either in particular cases or in general, directly or indirectly). Theistic inferentialists and theistic noninferentialists, for example, assume we can know that God would allow for there to be discoverable inferential and noninferential probabilifying evidence of his existence (respectively). Indeed, they assume that we can know what *kinds* of inferential and noninferential probabilifying evidence he would allow. For example, theistic inferentialist William Lane Craig assumes that we can know that God would cause a universe to be, theistic inferentialist Robin Collins assumes that we can know that God would create a fine-tuned universe containing a world that could support intelligent life, and theistic noninferentialist William Alston assumes that we can know that God would allow experiences of himself to be had by some of us. Theistic fideists, on the other hand, assume that we can know that God would *not* allow for there to be discoverable probabilifying evidence of his existence, that God would be pleased with our wagering on his existence (Pascal), that God would allow us to "have" him (Kierkegaard), and so on.

Of course, theistic philosophers are not the only ones who assume that we can know what God would do; atheistic philosophers (among others) do so as well, as is evidenced by their arguments for the nonexistence of God that involve a claim or set of claims about what God would do. For example, atheistic philosopher William Rowe assumes that God would not allow pointless evils.[1] And atheistic philosophers J. L. Schellenberg and Theodore Drange assume that God would make his existence more obvious to some of us.[2]

Perhaps none of this should come as a surprise. After all, many debates in the philosophy of religion, particularly those involving arguments for and against the existence of God, depend on a claim or set of claims about what God would do (again, in particular cases or in general, directly or indirectly). The debate on the problem of evil, for example, involves claims about:

- whether God would allow this or that natural evil to exist (particular and direct),
- whether God would allow any natural evil whatsoever to exist (general and direct),
- whether God would allow this or that moral evil to exist by allowing creatures with morally significant freedom to exist (particular and indirect),
- whether God would allow any moral evil whatsoever to exist by allowing creatures with morally significant freedom to exist (general and indirect).

And, it would be odd if not incoherent for theistic and atheistic philosophers to rely upon such claims if they did not first assume that we could know what God would do.

(Unless otherwise noted, I will write hereafter simply of what God would do without explicitly distinguishing between what God would do in particular cases or in general, directly or indirectly).

The list of debates and arguments that depend on a claim about what God would do could go on indefinitely. But, what is particularly noteworthy is that, despite the fact that theistic philosophers and their skeptical counterparts often disagree with one another about *what* God would do, they agree on this—that we can *know* what God would do.

Or do they? Certain theistic philosophers, to be referred to here as "skeptical theistic philosophers," doubt that we can know what God would do in some cases, particularly those involving horrendous and thereby seemingly pointless evils.[3] Consider, for example, William Rowe's version of the evidential argument from evil, an argument for the nonexistence of God based on the variety and profusion of evil in the world:

---

[1] William Rowe (2008), "The Inductive Argument from Evil Against the Existence of God," In Louis P. Pojman and Michael Rea (eds), *Philosophy of Religion: An Anthology*, 5th edition. Belmont, CA: Thomson Wadsworth, 200–7.

[2] J. L. Schellenberg (1993), *Divine Hiddenness and Human Reason*. Ithaca, NY: Cornell University Press.

[3] To my knowledge, Paul Draper coined the term "skeptical theist." See Paul Draper (1996), "The Skeptical Theist," In Daniel Howard-Snyder (ed.), *The Evidential Argument from Evil*. Bloomington, IN: Indiana University Press, 175–92.

P1: Probably, there are pointless evils.
P2: If God exists, there are no pointless evils.
C: Probably, God does not exist.[4]

The point of contention between the likes of Rowe, on the one hand, and skeptical theistic philosophers, on the other, lies with P1, since both proponents of the evidential argument from evil and theistic philosophers (skeptical or otherwise) tend to agree that God would not allow evils to be pointless, either in variety or profusion. Proponents of the evidential argument from evil hold that at least some evils are pointless—hence, P1. Skeptical theistic philosophers, however, hold that P1 has not been shown to be true. As Daniel Howard-Snyder argues, considerations about our cognitive limitations "constitute a good reason to be in doubt about whether it is highly likely that we would see a reason that would justify God in permitting so much evil if there were a reason."[5] For all we know, skeptical theistic philosophers submit, were we to know what God knows, we might know that God had no choice but to allow for the variety and profusion of the evil that we find in our world.

With this in mind, one can see that at the core of the debate on the evidential argument from evil is the question—is this or that horrendous evil pointless? In other words—is this or that horrendous evil *the sort of evil that God would not allow?* Skeptical theistic philosophers hold that we cannot know whether this or that horrendous evil is the sort of evil that God would not allow since, due to cognitive limitations, we cannot know whether this or that horrendous evil is evil *all things considered.* Skeptical theistic philosophers, then, do not agree that we can know what God would do, at least with respect to cases involving horrendous evil.

But, as Graham Oppy has argued, skeptical theism introduces a tension for theistic philosophers. He writes:

So, what's it to be? . . . If a nonbeliever is expected to accept that we have no idea whether it is likely that we'd see a reason justifying God in permitting horrendous evil, why on earth would you expect a nonbeliever to accept that we can see perfectly well that it is likely that we'd see a reason justifying God in creating a fine-tuned universe? Perhaps we nonbelievers might agree with Collins that the fact that it is good for intelligent, conscious beings to exist would provide God with a pro tanto . . . reason to create a world that could support intelligent life, just as we can surely insist that the fact that certain actions and events are horrendous evils would provide God with a pro tanto reason to prevent them. But why should we nonbelievers think that there is reason to have confidence about the move to an all-things-considered judgment in only one of these cases?

---

[4] William Rowe (2007), *Philosophy of Religion: An Introduction*, 4th edition. Belmont, CA: Wadsworth Publishing Company, 120.

[5] Daniel Howard-Snyder (1999), "God, Evil, and Suffering," In Michael J. Murray (ed.), *Reason for the Hope Within*. Grand Rapids, MI: Wm. B. Eerdmans Publishing, 112.

He continues:

> [William C.] Davis argues that "when all of the features of the world calling for explanation are taken together . . . the compelling verdict is that the world is much more the way one would have expected it to be given God's existence than it would have been if metaphysical naturalism were true." But, again, if we are to follow Howard-Snyder in accepting that we have good reason to be in doubt about whether it is highly likely that we would see all-things-considered reason that justifies God in permitting so much evil, why should we be prepared to follow Davis in supposing that we have no good reason to be in doubt about whether it is highly likely that we would see all-things-considered reason that justifies God in making a world like ours? Howard-Snyder clearly thinks that nonbelievers should concede that they are not well-placed to make judgments about what an omniscient and perfectly good being would permit (by way of horrendous evil); and Davis clearly thinks that nonbelievers should allow that they are well-enough placed to make judgments about the kind of universe that an omniscient and perfectly good being would create. I do not think that *any* Christian apologists can reasonably expect to have it both ways here.[6]

In addition to his central contention—that Christian apologists cannot reasonably expect to have it both ways—Oppy's remarks draw attention to the following—with regard to debates that depend on a claim about what God would do, before they can be resolved, we must first settle the more fundamental issue of whether we can know what God would do. For, until we do so, we cannot know whether God would allow for there to be inferential and/or noninferential probabilifying evidence of his existence, whether God would create a fine-tuned universe, whether God would allow horrendous evils, whether God would cause a universe to be, whether God would make his existence more obvious to some of us, and so on. And if we cannot know these things, then a problem arises for all three types of theistic philosopher (among others), for they assume that we *can* know what God would do. I refer to this as the "problem of skeptical theism."

In what follows, I lay out the possible answers to the problem of skeptical theism as well as their implications. Specifically, I contend that, with regard to whether we can know what God would do, three views exhaust the possibilities:

1. Broad skeptical theism—the view that, in every case, we cannot know what God would do.
2. Broad epistemic theism—the view that, in every case, we can know what God would do.
3. Narrow skeptical theism—the view that, in some cases, we can know what God would do and, in some cases, we cannot.

I then examine the implications of each of these views and argue that each presents serious problems for theistic philosophers. Specifically, I defend the following:

---

[6] Graham Oppy, review of *Reason for the Hope Within*, http://www.infidels.org/library/modern/graham_oppy/hope-within.html.

a. Given broad skeptical theism, theistic philosophers must relinquish all claims (explicit or implicit) about what God would do. This would cost theistic philosophers significantly, particularly the three types of theistic philosopher under consideration since all three rely upon claims about what God would do.
b. Given broad epistemic theism, theistic philosophers lose the principal grounds on which they reject P1 of the evidential argument from evil (above). Thus, unless theistic philosophers come up with a new, plausible objection to P1, they are left staking their case against the evidential argument from evil on evidential reasons for believing that God exists.
c. Given narrow skeptical theism, theistic philosophers must provide a plausible, principled distinction between those cases in which we can know what God would do and those cases in which we cannot. And, not only is their most commonly proposed principled distinction inadequate, it gives us reason to believe that narrow skeptical theism is too skeptical for its own good.

But, before examining the implications of each of these views, a word about "we" in statements such as "we can know what God would do" is in order.

By "we," I mean standard adult human beings (minimally), particularly theistic philosophers and their skeptical counterparts. After all, theistic and nontheistic philosophers make claims about what God would do while arguing with each other over God's existence. And what would be the point of making claims about what God would do if theistic philosophers did *not* assume that atheistic and agnostic philosophers can know what God would do? Similarly, what would be the point of making claims about what God would do if atheistic philosophers did *not* assume that theistic and agnostic philosophers can know what God would do? I, for one, cannot think of what the point of either of these possibilities would be; at least, not one of any philosophical import. By "we," then, I mean standard adult human beings, including both theistic and nontheistic philosophers.

On whether we can know what God would do

Implications of broad skeptical theism

As stated previously, broad skeptical theism is the view that, in every case, we cannot know what God would do. Embracing broad skeptical theism would cost theistic philosophers significantly since, in doing so, they could no longer rely upon claims about what God would do. In motivating the cost of embracing broad skeptical theism, I will focus on theistic inferentialists.

Embracing broad skeptical theism would require theistic inferentialists to relinquish every positive argument for God's existence, for a claim about what God would do may be derived from the premises of every positive argument for God's existence. That is, the premises of every positive argument for God's existence imply at least one claim about what God would do. Thus, if we cannot know what God would do à la broad skeptical theism, then we cannot know that God exists on the basis of positive arguments for his existence.[7]

Direct and indirect implication: An overview

There are two ways in which the premises of a positive argument for God's existence can imply a claim about what God would do—directly and indirectly. I shall address each of these ways in turn.

The premises of a positive argument for God's existence *directly* imply a claim about what God would do if a claim about what God would do may be derived from them, either immediately or after the following conceptual claims are added to the original argument:

> God Allows Claim (GAC)—If God exists and X exists or is the case, then God allows X to exist or be the case. (Or, in reference to the past—If God exists and X existed or was the case, then God allowed X to exist or be the case.)
> God Would Allow Claim (GWAC)—If God allows X to exist or be the case, then God would allow X to exist or be the case. (Or, in reference to the past—If God allowed X to exist or be the case, then God would have allowed X to exist or be the case.)[8]

By referring to these as conceptual claims, I mean to say that they are true or false (in this case, true) in virtue of their constitutive concepts. Regarding GAC, recall that by "God," we mean an omniscient, omnipotent, sovereign being (among other things); one who, as such, serves as the final arbiter of what things exist or are the case, at least with respect to that which is logically possible. Accordingly, if God exists and green cars exist, then God allows green cars to exist. Or, if God exists and dinosaurs existed, then God allowed dinosaurs to exist. So understood, one can see how GAC is true simply in virtue of its constitutive concepts.

Regarding GWAC, the "would" in this conditional claim is meant to express a likelihood. Accordingly, given GWAC, if God allows green cars to exist, then it is likely that God allows green cars to exist. In other words, if the likelihood of God allowing green cars to exist is 1, then the likelihood of God allowing green cars to exist is greater than 0.5. So understood, one can see how GWAC is true simply in virtue of its constitutive concepts.

An example of a positive argument for God's existence whose premises directly imply a claim about what God would do is as follows:

---

[7]   My argument depends on the assumption that knowledge is closed under known logical implication. For a critique of this view, see Fred Dretske (2005), "Is Knowledge Closed Under Known Entailment? The Case Against Closure," In Matthias Steup and Ernest Sosa (eds), *Contemporary Debates in Epistemology.* Oxford: Blackwell, 13–25.

[8]   Strictly speaking, adding *both* GAC and GWAC is not necessary—adding just GWAC would suffice, assuming one can get to GWAC without going through GAC.

P1: If some cars are green, then God exists.
P2: Some cars are green.
C1: God exists.

Given P1–C1, one may argue as follows:

C2: God exists and some cars are green.
P3: If God exists and some cars are green, then God allows some cars to be green.
(GAC)
C3: God allows some cars to be green.
P4: If God allows some cars to be green, then God would allow some cars to be
green. (GWAC)
C4: God would allow some cars to be green.

A claim about what God would do may be derived from the premises of the original
argument (P1–C1) after GAC and GWAC are added to it. Accordingly, the premises of
the original argument directly imply a claim about what God would do.

The premises of a positive argument for God's existence *indirectly* imply a claim
about what God would do, however, if a claim about what God would do may be derived
from it after adding to it the following intelligibility claim as well as the preceding
conceptual claims (GAC and GWAC):

Intelligibility Claim (IC)—We understand argument A (with "A" referring to the
argument in question).

An example of a positive argument for God's existence whose premises indirectly imply
a claim about what God would do is as follows:

P1: If God is perfect, then God exists.
P2: God is perfect.
C1: God exists.

Given P1–C1, one may argue as follows:

P3: We understand P1–C1. (IC)
C2: God exists and we understand P1–C1.
P4: If God exists and we understand P1–C1, then God allows us to understand
P1–C1. (GAC)
C3: God allows us to understand P1–C1.
P5: If God allows us to understand P1–C1, then God would allow us to understand
P1–C1. (GWAC)
C4: God would allow us to understand P1–C1.

A claim about what God would do may be derived from the premises of the original
argument (P1–C1) after IC, GAC, and GWAC are added to it. Accordingly, the premises
of the original argument indirectly imply a claim about what God would do.

Direct and indirect implication: Historical arguments

As for historical positive arguments for God's existence whose premises imply a claim about what God would do, let us first examine those whose premises directly imply such a claim. For practical purposes, I will restrict this examination to versions of three historical positive arguments for God's existence—the teleological, cosmological, and ontological arguments.

Consider, first, the following version of the teleological argument, attributable to Paley:

P1: Machines are produced by intelligent design.
P2: Many natural parts of the universe resemble machines.
C1: Probably, many natural parts of the universe are produced by intelligent design.
P3: Probably, God is the designer of the natural parts of the universe that resemble machines.
C2: Probably, God exists.[9]

Given P1–C2, one may argue as follows:

C3: Probably, God exists and, probably, God is the designer of the natural parts of the universe which resemble machines.
P4: If, probably, God exists and, probably, God is the designer of the natural parts of the universe which resemble machines, then, probably, God allows the natural parts of the universe which resemble machines to be designed. (GAC)
C4: Probably, God allows the natural parts of the universe which resemble machines to be designed.
P5: If, probably, God allows the natural parts of the universe resemble machines to be designed, then, probably, God would allow the natural parts of the universe that resemble machines to be designed. (GWAC)
C5: Probably, God would allow the natural parts of the universe that resemble machines to be designed.

Consider, next, the following version of the cosmological argument, attributable to Aquinas:

P1: There exist things that are caused to be.
P2: Nothing that is caused to be can be the cause of itself.
P3: There cannot be an infinite regress of causes.
C1: There exists an uncaused first cause of those things that are caused to be.
P4: Probably, God is the uncaused first cause of those things that are caused to be.
C2: Probably, God exists.[10]

9 P1–C1 are taken from Rowe, *Philosophy of Religion*, 55.
10 This is a modified version of an argument presented by Louis P. Pojman in *Philosophy of Religion: An Anthology*, 4th edition, ed. Louis J. Pojman. Belmont, CA: Thomson Wadsworth, 2003, 2.

Given P1–C2, one may argue as follows:

C3: Probably, God exists and, probably, God is the uncaused first cause of those things that are caused to be.

P5: If, probably, God exists and, probably, God is the uncaused first cause of those things that are caused to be, then, probably, God allows those things that are caused to be to exist. (GAC)

C4: Probably, God allows those things that are caused to be to exist.

P6: If, probably, God allows those things that are caused to be to exist, then, probably, God would allow those things that are caused to be to exist. (GWAC)

C5: Probably, God would allow those things that are caused to be to exist.

Finally, consider the following version of the ontological argument, attributable to Anselm:

P1: God—the greatest possible being—exists in the understanding.

P2: God might have existed in reality.

P3: If something exists only in the understanding and might have existed in reality, then it might have been greater than it is.

P4: Suppose God exists only in the understanding.

C1: God might have been greater than he is.

C2: God—the greatest possible being—is a being than which a greater is possible.

C3: It is not the case that God exists only in the understanding.

C4: God exists in reality as well as the understanding.[11]

Given P1–C4, one may argue as follows:

P5: If God exists in reality as well as the understanding, then God allows himself to exist in the understanding. (GAC)

C5: God allows himself to exist in the understanding.

P6: If God allows himself to exist in the understanding, then God would allow himself to exist in the understanding. (GWAC)

C6: God would allow himself to exist in the understanding.[12]

And so it goes with numerous other historical positive arguments for God's existence, such as the argument from miracles, the argument from religious experience, and the argument from morality.[13] Many historical positive arguments for God's existence, then, have premises that directly imply a claim about what God would do.

To be sure, it may not be that every historical positive argument for God's existence has premises that directly imply a claim about what God would do. But every historical

---

[11] This is a modified version of an argument found in Rowe, *Philosophy of Religion*, 41–2.

[12] Though this may sound odd to some, remember that God does not allow himself to exist in the understanding of the vast majority beings of which we are aware (dogs, cats, gorillas, etc.), or so it seems.

[13] For more examples, see Rob Lovering (2009), "On What God Would Do," *International Journal for Philosophy of Religion* 66(2): 95–6, footnote 11.

positive argument for God's existence has premises that indirectly imply a claim about what God would do. Indeed, the argument employed in my explanation of an argument whose premises indirectly imply a claim about what God would do is a version of the ontological argument. And it is worth mentioning a couple of others. Consider, for example, the following version of the argument from miracles, attributable to Swinburne:

P1: Extraordinary events occur.
P2: In some cases, these extraordinary events are not likely to have been the result of natural causes.
C1: In such cases, these extraordinary events are likely to have been the result of supernatural causes—that is, they are likely to have been miracles.
P3: Probably, God is the cause of extraordinary events that are likely to have been the result of supernatural causes.
C2: Probably, God exists.[14]

Given P1–C2, one may argue as follows:

P4: We understand P1–C2. (IC)
C3: Probably, God exists, and we understand P1–C2.
P5: If, probably, God exists, and we understand P1–C2, then, probably, God allows us to understand P1–C2. (GAC)
C4: Probably, God allows us to understand P1–C2.
P6: If, probably, God allows us to understand P1–C2, then, probably, God would allow us to understand P1–C2. (GWAC)
C5: Probably, God would allow us to understand P1–C2.

Consider, also, the following version of the argument from morality, attributable to C. S. Lewis:

P1: Moral laws exist.
P2: Moral laws must have been enacted by someone.
P3: Moral laws could not have been enacted by human beings.
C1: Moral laws must have been enacted by someone other than human beings.
P4: Probably, God is the one who enacted moral laws.
C2: Probably, God exists.[15]

Given P1–C2, one may argue as follows:

P5: We understand P1–C2. (IC)
C3: Probably, God exists, and we understand P1–C2.
P6: If, probably, God exists, and we understand P1–C2, then, probably, God allows us to understand P1–C2. (GAC)

---

[14] See Richard Swinburne (1996), *Is There a God?* New York, NY: Oxford University Press, 114ff.
[15] See C. S. Lewis (2001), *Mere Christianity.* San Francisco, CA: Harper San Francisco, 3ff.

C4: Probably, God allows us to understand P1–C2.

P7: If, probably, God allows us to understand P1–C2, then, probably, God would allow us to understand P1–C2. (GWAC)

C5: Probably, God would allow us to understand P1–C2.

And so it is with every other positive argument for God's existence, historical or other—each and every positive argument for God's existence is such that a claim about what God would do may be derived from its premises after adding IC, GAC, and GWAC to them. Accordingly, the premises of every positive argument for God's existence indirectly imply a claim about what God would do.

A claim about what God would do, then, is implied by the premises of every positive argument for God's existence, either directly, indirectly, or both. To rebut this, one would have to reject GAC, GWAC, or IC. Rejecting GAC and GWAC would involve rejecting conceptually true claims, and rejecting IC would entail that we do not understand any of the positive arguments for God's existence. Given this, it is unlikely that theistic inferentialists will reject GAC, GWAC, or IC. Bracketing the rejection of GAC, GWAC, or IC, then, were theistic inferentialists to embrace broad skeptical theism, they would have to relinquish every positive argument for God's existence, a costly choice indeed.

And, though I have focused on theistic inferentialists, it should be reiterated that embracing broad skeptical theism would cost theistic noninferentialists and theistic fideists as well. For doing so would require them to give up claims vital to their respective positions, such as the claim that God would allow experiences of himself to be had by some people (Alston and Swinburne), that God would be pleased with our wagering on his existence (Pascal), that God would allow us to "have" him (Kierkegaard), and so on. Embracing broad skeptical theism, then, would be very costly to theistic philosophers.

Implications of broad epistemic theism

Perhaps theistic philosophers should adopt broad epistemic theism—the view that, in every case, we can know what God would do. Were they to do so, they would avoid having to give up all claims about what God would do. Theistic philosophers would have to give up something else, however, something of great value to many of them—narrow skeptical theism. For, to embrace broad epistemic theism is to reject narrow skeptical theism. And rejecting narrow skeptical theism would cost theistic philosophers significantly as well, for narrow skeptical theism constitutes the principal grounds on which they object to the evidential argument from evil. As Richard Gale writes, ". . . by far the most favored response [to the evidential argument from evil] among sophisticated contemporary theorists, most notably Alston, Plantinga, Wykstra, and van Inwagen, is that of theistic skepticism" (what I am calling here narrow skeptical theism).[16]

---

[16] See Richard Gale (2007), *On the Philosophy of Religion*. Belmont, CA: Thomson Wadsworth, 105.

To see this, consider again P1 of Rowe's version of the evidential argument from evil—probably, there are pointless evils. Skeptical theistic philosophers reject P1 on the grounds that it depends on what is often referred to as the "noseeum assumption" —that, in the case of horrendous evil, we would very likely detect a greater good, if there were one. Skeptical theistic philosophers reject the noseeum assumption, embracing in its stead narrow skeptical theism. Specifically, skeptical theistic philosophers argue that we cannot know whether this or that horrendous evil is the sort of evil that God would not allow since, due to cognitive limitations, we cannot know whether this or that horrendous evil is evil *all things considered.*

But by embracing broad epistemic theism and thereby rejecting narrow skeptical theism, theistic philosophers would no longer have skeptical "for all we know" claims to raise against the noseeum assumption and, with it, P1. So, without narrow skeptical theism, theistic philosophers would lose the principal grounds on which they reject P1. Moreover, since theistic philosophers tend to accept P2, without these grounds, not only would the evidential argument from evil succeed, it would do so by theistic philosophers' own lights. At least, the evidential argument from evil would succeed by theistic philosophers' own lights until they do either one of two things—develop a new, plausible objection to P1 or come up with evidential reasons for believing that God exists that are strong enough to reject P1.

As of this writing, it appears that theistic philosophers have not developed a new, plausible objection to P1. That leaves theistic philosophers with coming up with evidential reasons for believing that God exists that are strong enough to reject P1. Before addressing this option, a little stage-setting is required.

Theistic philosophers would be correct to point out that, even without narrow skeptical theism, Rowe's evidential argument from evil can be rebutted. Indeed, Rowe himself recognizes that—despite the evidential argument from evil—theistic philosophers may be rationally justified in believing that God exists so long as they have even stronger evidential reasons for believing that God exists.[17] Specifically, Rowe acknowledges that theistic philosophers could pull what he calls a "G. E. Moore Shift." He describes this shift as follows—"We're given an argument: *p, q,* therefore, *r.* Instead of arguing directly against *p,* we construct another argument—not-*r, q,* therefore not-*p*—which begins with the denial of the conclusion of the first argument, keeps its second premise, and ends with the denial of the first premise as its conclusion."[18] Consider, again, Rowe's evidential argument from evil:

P1: Probably, there are pointless evils.
P2: If God exists, there are no pointless evils.
C: Probably, God does not exist.

Employing a G. E. Moore Shift, one gets:

P1*: Probably, God exists.

[17] Rowe, *Philosophy of Religion*, 130.
[18] Ibid., 128–9.

P2: If God exists, there are no pointless evils.
C*: Probably, there are no pointless evils.

And, as Rowe writes, "To the extent that she has stronger grounds for believing that the theistic God exists than for accepting [P1], the theist, on balance, may have more reason to reject [P1] than she does for accepting it."[19]

But this, of course, is not the end of the story. "However," Rowe continues, "in the absence of good reasons for believing that the theistic God exists, our study of the evidential form of the problem of evil has led us to the view that we are rationally justified in concluding that probably God does not exist."[20] All this to say, if theistic philosophers were to accept broad epistemic theism and, at the same time, successfully rebut the evidential argument from evil, they would need to possess evidential reasons for believing that God exists that are strong enough to reject P1. And, if what was discussed in Chapters 2 and 3 is any indication, coming up with such reasons will prove to be very difficult. Indeed, if such reasons were currently possessed, our continuing to debate the evidential argument from evil would be, for all intents and purposes, pointless. (Whether it would be pointlessly *evil*, I'll let you decide.)

A further problem with broad epistemic theism is that it entails that we can know much more about what God would do than theistic philosophers have traditionally thought we could know. For example, it would entail that we can know whether God would allow:

• the Boston Red Sox to win the World Series five years in a row
• all the world's active volcanoes to erupt at once
• coffee to be sold at a thousand dollars an ounce
• another Nazi holocaust to occur, and
• more than 100 angels to dance on the head of a pin

This will likely strike many theistic philosophers as implausible, since it narrows the gap between God's and our knowledge to an unseemly degree, making God out to be merely the most knowledgeable in a group of otherwise epistemic peers. And theistic philosophers tend to hold that the epistemic gap between God and us is much greater than that—indeed, for some theistic philosophers, the gap is best understood as one of kind rather than degree.

To sum up, were theistic philosophers to embrace broad epistemic theism, they would have to reject narrow skeptical theism. And rejecting narrow skeptical theism would cost theistic philosophers significantly, for narrow skeptical theism constitutes the principal grounds on which they object to the evidential argument from evil. Without it, without a replacement for it, or without even stronger evidential reasons for believing that God exists, the evidential problem of evil succeeds.

---

[19] Ibid., 130.
[20] Ibid.

Implications of narrow skeptical theism

If theistic philosophers reject both broad skeptical theism and broad epistemic theism, they are left with narrow skeptical theism—the view that, in some cases, we can know what God would do and, in some cases, we cannot. If narrow skeptical theism is to be plausible, however, a reason must be provided for thinking that we can know what God would do in some cases and not in others—simply declaring this to be the case will not suffice. And whatever the reason is, it should be rooted in a principled distinction between the cases. Skeptical theistic philosophers' most commonly proposed principled distinction is that cognitive limitations do not allow us to know what God would do in cases involving value (goodness/badness).[21] I will address this proposal and, in doing so, use as touchstones cases mentioned earlier in this chapter—Collins's case regarding a fine-tuned universe and Howard-Snyder's case regarding horrendous evils.

If we are not precluded from knowing what God would do in Collins's case while we are in Howard-Snyder's case, the question is—what is it about the former that allows us to know what God would do, and what is it about the latter that precludes us from knowing what God would do? What is the relevant difference between these two cases which generates the epistemic asymmetry constitutive of narrow skeptical theism? Well, Howard-Snyder's case requires our having comprehensive knowledge of when states of affairs are all-things-considered good and when they are all-things-considered bad or evil—comprehensive knowledge of the good, for short. Collins's case, on the other, does not require that we have comprehensive knowledge of the good, at least at first glance. And, according to skeptical theistic philosophers, we do not have comprehensive knowledge of the good. As Michael Bergmann puts it, "It just doesn't seem unlikely that our understanding of the realm of value falls miserably short of capturing all that is true about that realm."[22] For, to believe that we have comprehensive knowledge of the good is to believe:

a. that we have good reason for thinking that the possible goods we know of are representative of the possible goods there are;

b. that we have good reason for thinking that the possible evils we know of are representative of the possible evils there are;

c. that we have good reason for thinking that the entailment relations we know of between possible goods and the permission of possible evils are representative of the entailment relations there are between possible goods and the permission of possible evils; and,

---

[21] See Michael Bergmann (2001), "Skeptical Theism and Rowe's New Evidential Argument from Evil," *Nous* 35(2): 278–86.

[22] Ibid., 279.

d. that we have good reason for thinking that the total moral value or disvalue we perceive in certain complex states of affairs accurately reflects the total moral value or disvalue they really have.[23]

But, we do not have good reason for thinking anything of these things, or so Bergmann and other skeptical theistic philosophers contend; thus, we do not have good reason to believe that we have comprehensive knowledge of the good. Again, for all we know, were we to know what God knows, we might know that God had no choice but to allow for the variety and profusion of the evil that we find in our world. Skeptical theistic philosophers' proposed principled distinction, then, is that we are precluded from knowing what God would do in cases that require having comprehensive knowledge of the good, but not otherwise.

But, if skeptical theistic philosophers would have us be so skeptical about the good—about which we seem to know quite a bit, even if not comprehensively—then shouldn't they have us be equally, if not *more,* skeptical about the creation of universes, about which we know nothing at all? (To be sure, we may know a little about the beginning of a particular universe, but this is not one and the same as knowing about the creation of universes.) Specifically, in Collins's case, shouldn't skeptical theistic philosophers hold that, in order to conclude that a fine-tuned universe that contains a world that could support intelligent life is one that God would create, we would have to believe that we are in a position to determine when a given universe is more suited for creation than others? It seems they should, by parity of reasoning. And this would involve believing that we have good reason to think that the possible universes we know of are representative of the possible universes there are. But, we don't have good reason for thinking that the possible universes we know of are representative of the possible universes there are—at least, we have no more reason for thinking this than for thinking that the possible goods we know of are representative of the possible goods there are. Indeed, for all we know, were we to know what God knows, we might know that God would have had no choice but to create a universe that *wasn't* fine-tuned, one that *didn't* include a world that could support intelligent life.[24] Paraphrasing David Hume, a very small part of this great universe, during a very short time, is very imperfectly discovered to us; and do we thence pronounce decisively concerning all the ways it might have been?

---

[23] See Michael Bergmann (2009), "Skeptical Theism and the Problem of Evil," In T. P. Thomas and M. Rea (eds), *The Oxford Handbook of Philosophical Theology.* Oxford: Oxford University Press, 376ff. It should be noted that there are stronger and weaker formulations of skeptical theism. As Stephen Maitzen writes, "skeptical theists sometimes adopt the strong line that we should expect God's morally sufficient reasons to be inscrutable and sometimes the weaker line that we should not expect to [sic] those reasons to be scrutable" (Stephen Maitzen (2007), "Skeptical Theism and God's Commands," *Sophia* 46: 235). The formulation under consideration is of the weaker sort. For an example of the stronger formulation, see Stephen Wykstra (1984), "The Humean Obstacle to Evidential Arguments from Suffering: On Avoiding Evils of 'Appearance,'" *International Journal for Philosophy of Religion* 16: 73–93.

[24] Of course, if this were the case, then we would have reason to believe that God does not exist.

The second reason this proposed principled distinction—that we are precluded from knowing what God would do in cases that require having comprehensive knowledge of the good, but not otherwise—will not suffice is that, contrary to what has been assumed up to this point, Collins's case *does* require having comprehensive knowledge of the good. His own defense of what kind of universe God would create makes this clear—"Since God is an all good being, and *it is good* for intelligent, conscious beings to exist, it is not surprising or improbable that God would create a world that could support intelligent life."[25] As one can see, Collins's case requires having comprehensive knowledge of the good as it involves not only the explicit claim that it is all-things-considered good for intelligent, conscious beings to exist, but also the implicit claim that a fine-tuned universe that includes a world that could support intelligent life is a good one, all things considered.

Of course, Collins does not employ the locution "all things considered," but surely this is implied. After all, the alternative interpretation is that Collins is simply claiming that it is good for intelligent, conscious beings to exist, *all else being equal*. But if Collins is simply making an all-else-being-equal claim, then it remains possible that it is *bad* for intelligent, conscious beings to exist, all things considered. Needless to say, this would render Collins's fined-tuned-universe defense of God's existence unsound. For, from the mere fact that a state of affairs is good, all else being equal, it does not follow that it is good or even probably good, all things considered. In turn, it does not follow that, probably, God would create such a state of affairs. Indeed, this seems to be the very point that skeptical theistic philosophers have made regarding the evidential argument from evil—from the mere fact that a state of affairs is evil, all else being equal, it does not follow that it is evil or even probably evil, all things considered. The most charitable interpretation of Collins, then, is that he is making all-things-considered claims.

Narrow skeptical theism—too skeptical for its own good

Some might respond to the preceding by arguing that, though *Collins's* case depends on having comprehensive knowledge of the good, it does not follow that every other case does as well. And, if other cases do not depend on having comprehensive knowledge of the good, skeptical theistic philosophers' proposed principled distinction remains in play. There are at least two problems with this response.

First, many cases involve goodness/badness at one level or another. Obviously, a salient feature of cases involving horrendous evils—a feature that is doing much of the probabilifying work with respect to God's existence—is that of goodness/badness. The rest is, for all intents and purposes, conceptual garnish. One of Rowe's famous cases of horrendous evil involves the suffering of a terminally burned fawn, but it might as well have involved the suffering of a terminally frostbitten wolf. For it is not the kind of being that is suffering or the physical cause of the suffering that is doing the probabilifying work with respect to God's existence, but the goodness/badness of the suffering—the

<hr>

[25] Robin Collins, "A Scientific Argument for the Existence of God," in *Philosophy of Religion: An Anthology*, 78, emphasis mine.

suffering is deemed by some philosophers to be all-things-considered bad, and others to be all-things-considered good (or, at least, not so bad).[26]

In addition, there are cases that do not involve horrendous evils in which goodness/ badness is nevertheless a salient feature. Take cases involving the hiddenness of God, cases involving (in Schellenberg's words) "the absence of some kind of positive experiential result in the search for God."[27] In such cases, a salient feature is that of goodness/badness. For, the absence of some kind of positive experiential result in the search for God is deemed by some philosophers to be all-things-considered bad, and others to be all-things-considered good (or, at least, not so bad).[28] Or, take cases involving morally significant freedom (à la the soul-making defense of God's hiddenness). Once again, in such cases, a salient feature is that of goodness/badness. For that human beings have morally significant freedom is deemed by some philosophers to be all-things-considered good, and others to be all-things-considered bad (or, at least, not so good).[29]

Finally, there are cases in which goodness/badness is not a salient feature but, nevertheless, is among the cases' features. Both cases involving religious experiences and cases involving miracles, for example, typically include goodness/badness among their features, as such events are deemed by some philosophers to be all-things-considered good (or, at least, not bad). Many cases, then, involve goodness/badness at one level or another.

But, there is an even bigger problem with the preceding response—it overlooks that what God would do in *any* case will have to be compatible with, if not determined by, his perfect goodness. From the broadest case regarding what God would do—the case of what kind of universe(s), down to the smallest of details, God would create—to the narrowest of cases—such as cases of whether God would perform a miracle in this situation or allow evil in that situation—each will have to be compatible with God's perfect goodness. Thus, knowing what God would do in *any* case requires having comprehensive knowledge of the good. For, if we lack comprehensive knowledge of the good, then we cannot know (for example) whether God's hiddenness is compatible with his perfect goodness; thus, we cannot know whether God would or would not be hidden. Or, if we lack comprehensive knowledge of the good, then we cannot know

---

[26] Rowe thinks the suffering is all-things-considered bad, of course, while skeptical theistic philosophers are not convinced of this.

[27] J. L. Schellenberg (2004), "Does Divine Hiddenness Justify Atheism?," In Michael L. Peterson and Raymond J. VanArragon (eds), *Contemporary Debates in Philosophy of Religion*. Oxford: Blackwell Publishing, 31.

[28] For example, J. L. Schellenberg thinks the absence of some kind of positive experiential result in the search for God is bad, while Michael J. Murray thinks it is, at least, not so bad. See Schellenberg, *Divine Hiddenness and Human Reason*; and Michael J. Murray (2002), "Deus Absconditus," In Daniel Howard-Snyder and Paul K. Moser (eds), *Divine Hiddenness: New Essays*. Cambridge: Cambridge University Press, 62–82.

[29] For example, Michael J. Murray thinks free will is good, while David Lewis thinks free will is, at least, not nearly as good as some theistic philosophers make it out to be. See Michael J. Murray (1993), "Coercion and the Hiddenness of God," *American Philosophical Quarterly* 30(1), 27–38; and David Lewis (2009), "Divine Evil," In Kevin Timpe (ed.), *Arguing About Religion*. New York, NY: Routledge, 472–81.

whether the existence of intelligent, conscious beings is compatible with God's perfect goodness; thus, we cannot know whether God would or would not create intelligent, conscious beings. And so on. If, then, in an attempt to defend narrow skeptical theism, theistic philosophers were to accept this proposed principled distinction—that we are precluded from knowing what God would do in cases that require having comprehensive knowledge of the good, but not otherwise—then we could never know what God would do and *broad* skeptical theism would be true. If we are to know what God would do in any case, then, we must have comprehensive knowledge of the good. Yet—and here's the rub—skeptical theistic philosophers *deny* that we have comprehensive knowledge of the good. Narrow skeptical theism, it appears, is too skeptical for its own good.

Conclusion

I have argued that, with respect to the issue of whether we can know what God would do, there are three possibilities:

1. Broad skeptical theism—The view that, in every case, we cannot know what God would do.
2. Broad epistemic theism—The view that, in every case, we can know what God would do.
3. Narrow skeptical theism—The view that, in some cases, we can know what God would do and, in some cases, we cannot.

I have also argued that each view has troubling implications for all three types of theistic philosopher. Specifically, I have argued that:

a. Given broad skeptical theism, theistic philosophers must relinquish all claims (explicit or implicit) about what God would do. This would cost theistic philosophers significantly, particularly the three types of theistic philosopher under consideration as all three rely upon claims about what God would do.
b. Given broad epistemic theism, theistic philosophers lose the principal grounds on which they reject P1 of the evidential argument from evil (above). Thus, unless theistic philosophers come up with a new, plausible objection to P1, they are left staking their case against the evidential argument from evil on evidential reasons for believing that God exists.
c. Given narrow skeptical theism, theistic philosophers must provide a plausible, principled distinction between those cases in which we can know what God would do and those cases in which we cannot. And, not only is their most commonly proposed principled distinction inadequate, it gives us reason to believe that narrow skeptical theism is too skeptical for its own good.

If this is correct, theistic philosophers are in the unenviable position of having to decide among three unsavory views on this fundamental issue.

6

Another Problem for All Three Theistic Philosophers

Introduction

In the previous chapter, I argued that all three types of theistic philosopher share a problem—the problem of skeptical theism. A second problem they all share is the belief that God—as essentially omniscient, omnipotent, and perfectly good—is a logically possible being. Many philosophers have attempted to demonstrate that this is false, usually by way of arguing that it is logically impossible for something to be essentially omniscient and/or essentially omnipotent and/or essentially perfectly good. In this chapter, I follow this strategy, arguing that it is logically impossible for God to be essentially omniscient. I refer to this as the "problem of divine omniscience." I present two arguments for this, the difference between the two being the understanding of omniscience at work. In the first argument, by "omniscience," I mean maximal propositional knowledge as well as maximal experiential knowledge. In the second argument, by "omniscience," I mean simply maximal propositional knowledge. On either understanding, I argue that it logically impossible for God to be essentially omniscient.

On the logical impossibility of divine omniscience—first argument

Key concepts and assumptions

The key concepts of the first argument are:

- propositional knowledge (and, with it, maximal propositional knowledge)
- temporally variant and invariant propositions
- experiential knowledge (and, with it, maximal experiential knowledge), and
- omniscience

Each will be discussed in turn.

Regarding propositional knowledge and experiential knowledge, a thorough discussion of the natures of these concepts as well as what, precisely, distinguishes them is beyond the scope of this chapter.[1] The following, then, will have to suffice.

By "propositional knowledge," I mean knowledge of the truth-values of propositions. Statements in the form "*S* knows the truth-value of *p*" and "*S* does not know the truth-value of *p*"—where *S* stands for an individual possessing the capacity for knowledge and *p* stands for a proposition—are to be understood as statements of propositional knowledge. For example, "Joe knows the truth-value of 'Barack Obama is President of the United States' " is a statement of propositional knowledge.

This brings us to the distinction between temporally variant and temporally invariant propositions.[2] By temporally variant propositions, I mean propositions whose truth-values change with time; while by temporally invariant propositions, I mean propositions whose truth-values do not change with time. The proposition "Something is what it is" is a temporally invariant proposition. The proposition "Barack Obama is President of the United States," however, is a temporally variant proposition: as of this writing, it has a truth-value of *true*; thirty years ago, it had a truth-value of *false*. That said, the understanding of propositional knowledge at work here is knowledge of the truth-values of both temporally variant and temporally invariant propositions.

With this understanding of propositional knowledge in mind, by maximal propositional knowledge, I mean knowledge of all the truth-values of all the propositions—temporally variant or invariant—it is logically possible to know.[3] (In Chapter 2, I acknowledged Michael Tooley's challenge to the coherence of some maximal properties. If maximal propositional knowledge is incoherent, then God cannot possess it.)

By experiential knowledge, I mean knowledge of things other than propositions, such as knowledge of what it is like to engage in a particular activity, of what it is like to experience a particular emotion, of what it is like to experience a particular state of affairs, and so on. Statements in the form "*S* knows what it is like to *x*" and "*S* does not know what it is like to *x*"—where *x* stands for an activity, the experiencing of an emotion, the experiencing of a state of affairs, or anything else that may be known experientially—are to be understood as statements of experiential knowledge. That said, by "maximal experiential knowledge," I mean knowledge of all that it is logically possible to know experientially.

As for omniscience, I will rely upon two understandings of the concept. One understanding is maximal propositional knowledge; the other is maximal propositional

---

[1] A good place to start is Richard Fumerton's "Experiential Knowledge and Description," at http://plato.stanford.edu/entries/knowledge-acquaindescrip/. For an argument that propositional knowledge and experiential knowledge are not distinguishable, see Anthony Kenny (1989), *The Metaphysics of the Mind*. Oxford: Oxford University Press, 110; and Anthony Kenny (1979), *The God of the Philosophers*. Oxford: Oxford University Press, 30.

[2] Thanks to Thomas Flint for recommending the inclusion of this distinction.

[3] There is disagreement among philosophers whether such an understanding of maximal propositional knowledge is consistent with divine simplicity. For more on the nature of this disagreement, see Norman Kretzmann (1966), "Omniscience and Immutability," *Journal of Philosophy* 63: 409–21.

as well as maximal experiential knowledge (maximal propositional/experiential knowledge, for short).[4] It is the latter understanding of omniscience that will be relied upon in this first argument (though the former understanding will be given due consideration, both in the present discussion as well as in the discussion of my second argument for the logical impossibility of divine omniscience). And, since omniscience is understood to be one of God's essential properties, God is understood not only to possess maximal propositional/experiential knowledge, but to have always possessed it.

Having addressed some of the key concepts of this section, let us turn our attention to two of the key assumptions. Both assumptions will be examined critically as the chapter progresses, but it should be noted now that the first may be derived from the understanding of omniscience under consideration—maximal propositional/experiential knowledge. The key assumptions are as follows:

A1: Necessarily, if S is essentially omniscient, then there is not a time t during S's existence at which (i) S does not know the truth-value of a proposition or (ii) S does not know what it is like not to know the truth-value of a proposition.

A2: Necessarily, if S knows what it is like not to know the truth-value of a proposition, then there is a time t during S's existence at which S does not know the truth-value of a proposition.

(NB: Not knowing what it is like not to know the truth-value of a proposition is not knowing what it is like not to know the truth-value of any proposition whatsoever.) Objections to these assumptions will be considered in due course.[5]

The argument

It is not possible for God to be essentially omniscient—that is, it is not possible for God to possess maximal propositional/experiential knowledge and to have always done so, or so I shall argue. For, briefly, if God has always possessed maximal propositional knowledge, then there is a time t at which God does not possess maximal experiential knowledge; while if God has always possessed maximal experiential knowledge, then there is a time t at which God does not possess maximal propositional knowledge.

To see this, consider the proposition, p—"God knows what it is like not to know the truth-value of a proposition." If p is true, then there is a time t during God's existence at which God does not know the truth-value of a proposition and, thus, God is not essentially omniscient. To see this clearly, consider the following:

---

[4] For example, Richard Gale adopts the former understanding (see Richard Gale (2007), *On the Philosophy of Religion*. Belmont, CA: Thomson Wadsworth, 13); while Thomas V. Morris adopts the latter understanding (see Thomas V. Morris (2003), "Omnipotence and Omniscience," In Charles Taliaferro and Paul J. Griffiths (eds), *Philosophy of Religion*. Malden, MA: Blackwell Publishing, 65).

[5] By "necessarily," I have metaphysical necessity in mind; while by a "time" t, I mean physical, if not metaphysical, time.

P1: God knows what it is like not to know the truth-value of a proposition. (*p*)

P2: Necessarily, if God knows what it is like not to know the truth-value of a proposition, then there is a time *t* during God's existence at which God does not know the truth-value of a proposition. (A2)

C1: There is a time *t* during God's existence at which God does not know the truth-value of a proposition.

P3: Necessarily, if God is essentially omniscient, then there is not a time *t* during God's existence at which (i) God does not know the truth-value of a proposition or (ii) God does not know what it is like not to know the truth-value of a proposition. (A1)

C2: God is not essentially omniscient.

So, again, if *p* is true, then there is a time *t* during God's existence at which God does not know the truth-value of a proposition and, thus, God is not essentially omniscient.

If, on the other hand, *p* is false, then, once again, God is not essentially omniscient. To see this clearly, consider the following:

P1: God does not know what it is like not to know the truth-value of a proposition. (~*p*)

P2: Necessarily, if God is essentially omniscient, then there is not a time *t* during God's existence at which (i) God does not know the truth-value of a proposition or (ii) God does not know what it is like not to know the truth-value of a proposition. (A1)

C: God is not essentially omniscient.

So, if *p* is false, then there is a time *t* during God's existence at which God does not know what it is like not to know the truth-value of a proposition and, thus, God is not essentially omniscient.

To sum up, the understanding of God's omniscience under consideration is maximal propositional/experiential knowledge. Either God knows what it is like not to know the truth-value of a proposition or he does not. And, either way, it follows that God is not—indeed, cannot be—essentially omniscient.

Possible solutions

There are two possible solutions that I would like to discuss here, and they may be distinguished in the following way—one solution retains the understanding of omniscience as maximal propositional/experiential knowledge (for the most part, anyway), while the other forgoes this understanding and restricts omniscience to maximal propositional knowledge. (I refer to this latter understanding as the "restricted sense of omniscience.") Each solution will be examined in turn.

Regarding the first solution, one could modify the understanding of God's omniscience by construing it in terms of maximal propositional and *nearly* maximal experiential knowledge, with the latter meant to convey that God has experiential knowledge of everything, save for what it is like not to know the truth-value of a proposition (at a time *t*). An immediately identifiable problem with this solution, however, is that one could just as easily modify the understanding of God's omniscience by construing it in terms of maximal experiential and *nearly* maximal propositional knowledge, with the latter meant to convey that God has propositional knowledge of everything save for one proposition (at a time *t*). And it is not at all clear which solution is preferable (if either solution *is* preferable—after all, either way, God would lack maximal knowledge of one sort or another). Whatever it is, it will have to be the one that, among other things, renders God the greater being, since God is understood here to be the greatest actual, if not the greatest possible, being. So, assuming both propositional knowledge and experiential knowledge are great-making qualities (an assumption to be addressed shortly), the question is—which God is greater? The God who possesses maximal propositional and nearly maximal experiential knowledge, or the God who possesses maximal experiential and nearly maximal propositional knowledge? For present purposes, I will simply submit that I haven't the faintest idea which God is greater. What's more, I do not see how anyone could have much confidence in any answer that may be proffered, as there are so many other seemingly intractable issues one would need to address before one can adequately answer this question.

For example, one would need to address the extent to which propositional knowledge and experiential knowledge are great-making qualities as well as whether the great-making quality of propositional knowledge is greater than the great-making quality of experiential knowledge (or vice versa). And doing this would be no mean feat, as it would involve answering questions such as:

- Is propositional knowledge equally great-making regardless of what is known propositionally, or is some propositional knowledge more great-making than other propositional knowledge?
- Is experiential knowledge equally great-making regardless of what is known experientially, or is some experiential knowledge more great-making than other experiential knowledge?
- To what extent is knowing the truth-value of, say, "Some dogs are blind" a great-making quality?
- To what extent is knowing what it is like, say, to surf a great-making quality?
- Is knowing the truth-value of "Some dogs are blind" a *greater* great-making quality than knowing the truth-value of "Some people dislike their siblings"?
- Is knowing what it is like to surf a *greater* great-making quality than knowing what it is like to love someone?
- Is knowing the truth-value of "Some dogs are blind" a *greater* great-making quality than knowing what it is like to surf?
- What renders God greater—possessing maximal propositional knowledge and nearly maximal experiential knowledge *save for* knowing what it is like to surf, or possessing maximal experiential knowledge and nearly maximal propositional knowledge *save for* knowing the truth-value of "Some dogs are blind"?

With questions such as these to be answered, I simply do not see how anyone could have much confidence in any answer that may be proffered to the question—which God is greater—the God who possesses maximal propositional and nearly maximal experiential knowledge, or the God who possesses maximal experiential and nearly maximal propositional knowledge? Indeed, there may be no fact to the matter.

Regarding the second solution, one could reject the view that God's omniscience is best understood in terms of maximal propositional/experiential knowledge and, instead, adopt the restricted sense of omniscience. In so doing, one would be rejecting A1, since experiential knowledge is constitutive of A1. But restricting God's omniscience to maximal propositional knowledge produces problems of its own.

First, unless there is good reason to restrict the concept of omniscience to maximal propositional knowledge, it seems the concept of omniscience should include all varieties of knowledge. The question, then, is whether there is good reason to restrict the concept of omniscience to maximal propositional knowledge. If there is, it has yet to be sufficiently articulated, as philosophers who restrict it in this way usually do so by stipulation. Consider, for example, the following passage regarding God's omniscience:

> If we return to the issue of divine omniscience, we can see that there may be a problem with attributing [experiential knowledge] to God . . . given that God is (arguably) impassable and therefore not affected by anything, then how could he know what sadness feels like? . . . We'll leave these cases for you to think about for yourself, since most philosophical attention has been directed towards the nature and extent of God's *propositional knowledge*.[6]

Notice that the authors of this passage acknowledge experiential knowledge and, specifically, that it may indeed be constitutive of God's omniscience. Notice also, however, that they leave the matter at that, preferring to construe God's omniscience in terms of mere propositional knowledge "since most philosophical attention" has been directed toward this understanding of omniscience. Their doing so is not without cause, for most philosophical attention *has* been directed toward the restricted sense of omniscience.[7]

Second, there is at least one reason—and a compelling one at that—to include experiential knowledge in the understanding of God's omniscience. Consider that if God's knowledge is restricted to propositional knowledge, then it is possible for there to be a being greater than God, namely, a being who shares all of God's great-making qualities—including maximal propositional knowledge—*plus* the great-making quality

---

[6] Beverley Clack and Brian Clack (2008), *The Philosophy of Religion: A Critical Introduction*. 2nd edition. Cambridge: Polity, 63.

[7] Similarly, in his article "The Divine Attributes," Nicholas Everitt restricts the concept of omniscience to maximal propositional knowledge by stipulation—"Must an omniscient being know everything? A first qualification is to set aside the so-called 'knowledge how to,' and knowledge by acquaintance, and to restrict omniscience to propositional knowledge" (Nicholas Everitt (2010), "The Divine Attributes," *Philosophy Compass* 5: 81).

of experiential knowledge. But, God is understood here to be the greatest actual, if not the greatest possible, being. Assuming a greatest possible being is indeed possible, then, God must possess experiential knowledge in addition to maximal propositional knowledge. And, it would be odd, if not incoherent, not to count God's experiential knowledge as constitutive of his omniscience.

Now, someone might object to my contention that such a being would be greater than God on the grounds that experiential knowledge is not a great-making quality. But, arguably, this would be a mistake. As Joshua Hoffman and Gary Rosenkrantz state, "Whether a particular quality should be included in a set of great-making qualities depends on the nature of the pertinent category."[8] In the case of God, the pertinent category is that of *entity* and, as such, "the relevant great-making qualities pertain to an entity's *worthiness for worship and moral admiration*."[9] (Lest there be any misunderstanding, "worship" means (minimally) reverence or adoration. I will use reverence or adoration throughout to avoid confusion.) And, there is reason to think that experiential knowledge makes an entity more worthy of reverence and moral admiration than it otherwise would be.

To begin with, it is hard to see why having maximal propositional knowledge would contribute to an entity's worthiness for reverence and moral admiration—as most proponents of the restricted sense of omniscience believe it does—while having experiential knowledge would not. As indicated above, experiential knowledge differs from propositional knowledge with respect to the kinds of things that are known (and, at least in part, the way in which these things come to be known). In the case of propositional knowledge, what is known are propositions; while in the case of experiential knowledge, what is known are things other than propositions. But, in both cases, something is known, and it is hard to believe that whether knowledge is a great-making quality turns entirely on the *kinds* of things that are known—specifically, on whether what is known is propositional or nonpropositional in nature—and not simply *that* something is known as well.

To motivate this point, consider a possible entity, *E*, which may exist in one of two ways—*E* possesses propositional knowledge of leadership (what it means to be a leader, what the capacity to lead involves, etc.), but no experiential knowledge of leadership whatsoever, or *E* possesses propositional knowledge of leadership *plus* experiential knowledge of leadership. In the first scenario, *E* is "book smart" when it comes to leadership, but not "street smart," if you will, while in the second scenario, *E* is both book smart and street smart. That the kinds of things that are known about leadership experientially are different from the kinds of things that are known about leadership propositionally seems insufficient for determining whether *E*'s overall greater knowledge of leadership in the latter case makes *E* more worthy of reverence and moral admiration. What seems relevant as well is *that* something is known about leadership, propositionally or otherwise. Furthermore, *E*'s possession of experiential

<hr />

[8] Joshua Hoffman and Gary S. Rosenkrantz (2002), *The Divine Attributes*. New York, NY: Blackwell, 15.
[9] Hoffman and Rosenkrantz, 16.

knowledge of leadership seems to make *E* greater—more worthy of reverence and moral admiration—than *E* otherwise would be.

One might object to the preceding by claiming that experiential knowledge of leadership makes *E* greater qua *leader*, but not qua *entity*. But this is implausible, particularly if one believes that having propositional knowledge of leadership makes an entity greater than it otherwise would be. To see this, consider God again. As omniscient, God has maximal propositional knowledge, which includes propositional knowledge of leadership, among other things. (Without propositional knowledge of leadership, after all, God would not have maximal propositional knowledge and, in turn, would not be omniscient.) And God's having maximal propositional knowledge makes him greater qua entity than he otherwise would be, or so most proponents of the restricted sense of omniscience believe. Yet, if God's having maximal propositional knowledge—which includes propositional knowledge of leadership— renders him greater qua entity than he otherwise would be, why wouldn't his having knowledge of what it is like to be a leader also make him greater qua entity than he otherwise would be? There seems to be no principled reason for thinking it would not. What's more, there is at least one compelling reason to think that it would—we have more reverence and moral admiration for those who have led and thereby know what it is like to lead than for those who simply have propositional knowledge about leadership. Consider, for example, the reverence and moral admiration we have for the likes of George Washington and Winston Churchill versus the likes of newly minted graduates of West Point or the Naval Academy. And the reverence and moral admiration we have for individuals who have led and thereby know what it is like to lead is qua entity, not simply qua leader—though, to be sure, our reverence and moral admiration for them qua leader contributes to our reverence and moral admiration for them qua entity.

(It should be added that having reverence and moral admiration for *E* qua entity in virtue of *E*'s experiential knowledge of what it is like to lead does not entail having reverence and moral admiration for *E* qua entity *full stop*. In some cases, in addition to the great-making quality of experiential knowledge of leadership, *E* possesses a whole host of bad-making qualities, which renders *E*—qua entity—unworthy of reverence and moral admiration, all things considered.)

To sum up, one possible solution to my argument for the logical impossibility of divine omniscience is to modify the understanding of omniscience by construing it in terms of maximal propositional and nearly maximal experiential knowledge. A problem with this solution is that one could just as easily modify the understanding of omniscience by construing it in terms of maximal experiential and nearly maximal propositional knowledge, and it is not at all clear which solution is preferable (if either is) since, among other things, it is not at all clear which possibility renders God the greater being. Another possible solution is to reject A1 and, instead, adopt the restricted sense of omniscience. But, if experiential knowledge is a great-making quality—as arguably it is—then understanding God's omniscience in the restricted sense would entail that God is *not* the greatest possible being, assuming a greatest possible being is indeed possible.

Objections to the first argument

One objection has already been addressed above, namely, the objection to A1. Three more objections I would like to discuss pertain to (a) A2, (b) whether *all* experiential knowledge is great-making and (c) whether there really *is* something that it is like not to know the truth-value of a proposition.

Objections to A2—round one

As for objections to A2, there are quite a few. As a result, I shall cover them in two rounds, grouped (roughly) by type.

Perhaps the most efficient way to respond to objections to A2 is to cut to the chase and consider the implications of A2 being false. If A2 is false, then it is possible for S to know what it is like not to know the truth-value of a proposition despite S having always known all the truth-values of all the propositions it is logically possible to know. But it is hard to see how this could be the case. To begin with, S could not know what it is like not to know the truth-value of a proposition by not knowing the truth-value of a proposition it is logically possible to know since, *ex hypothesi*, S has always known all the truth-values of all the propositions it is logically possible to know. If S is to know what it is like not to know the truth-value of a proposition, then, it must be by not knowing the truth-value of a proposition that it is logically *impossible* for S to know. So, what might be an example of such a proposition?

One might think that contradictory propositions are propositions the truth-values of which it is logically impossible for S to know. But this would be a mistake, as it is logically possible for S to know the truth-values of contradictory propositions, according to both classical and nonclassical logics.[10]

One might also think that nonsensical propositions—such as "The color of C major is anger"—are propositions the truth-values of which it is logically impossible for S to know. But, once again, this would be a mistake, for nonsensical propositions are not genuine propositions; they are pseudo propositions. Genuine propositions are the kinds of things that, in principle, can have truth-values, and nonsensical propositions such as the "The color of C major is anger" are not such things.

One might think that propositions contained in a Wittgensteinian private language are propositions the truth-values of which it is logically impossible for S to know for all Ss not identical with the possessor of the private language.[11] Assuming (contra Wittgenstein) private languages are possible *and* that propositions contained

---

[10] For truth-values of contradictions according to classical logic, see Patrick Hurley (2011), *A Concise Introduction to Logic*, 11th edition. Belmont, CA: Wadsworth Publishing. For truth-values of contradictions according to non-classical logics, see Graham Priest (2001), *An Introduction to Non-Classical Logic*. Cambridge: Cambridge University Press.

[11] As Wittgentstein describes a private language, "The words of this language are to refer to what can be known only to the speaker; to his immediate, private, sensations. So another cannot understand the language" (See Ludwig Wittgenstein (1953), *Philosophical Investigations*, trans. G. E. M. Anscombe. Oxford: Blackwell, 253).

therein are propositions the truth-values of which it is logically impossible for S to know for all Ss not identical with the possessor of the private language, it is not clear how Ss not identical with the possessor of the private language *could* know what it is like not to know the truth-values of such propositions. For S to know what it is like not to know the truth-values of propositions contained in someone else's private language, S would have to mentally entertain those propositions somehow. But, how could that ever occur, given that these propositions are constitutive of someone else's *private* language? To be sure, S may be able to mentally entertain the sentence that captures the privately known proposition—perhaps the owner of the private language could spell it out for S as "Ohhdnt skloiaen doiot." But how could S mentally entertain the private proposition captured by that sentence? I do not see how S ever could.

Finally, one might think that propositions involving essential indexicals are propositions the truth-values of which it is logically impossible for S to know. Take the proposition "I am typing at this moment" with the "I" referring to this author, Rob Lovering. One might think it is logically impossible for S to know the truth-value of this proposition for all Ss not numerically identical with the individual referred to by "I." More specifically, one might argue that "I am typing at this moment" and "Rob Lovering is typing at this moment" do not express the same proposition, and that it is logically impossible for S to know the truth-value of the proposition "I am typing at this moment" for all Ss not numerically identical with the individual referred to by "I."

Among others, Patrick Grim argues along these lines. He asks us to consider a case in which he is making a mess in a supermarket. He asks us then to consider whether "I am making a mess" and "Patrick Grim is making a mess" express the same proposition. Do they? Grim thinks not. He writes,

> When I stop myself short in the supermarket, gather up my broken sack, and start to tidy up, this may be quite fully explained by saying that I realize (or come to believe, or come to know) that I am making a mess—what I express by ["I am making a mess"]. But it cannot be fully explained, or at least as fully explained, by saying that I realize that Patrick Grim is making a mess—what is expressed by ["Patrick Grim is making a mess"]. In order to give a realization on my part that Patrick Grim is making a mess the full explanatory force of my realization that *I* am making a mess, in fact, we would have to add that I know that *I* am Patrick Grim.[12]

And that, of course, is something only Ss numerically identical with Patrick Grim could know.[13]

---

[12] Patrick Grim (2003), "Against Omniscience: The Case from Essential Indexicals," In Michael Martin and Ricki Monnier (eds), *The Impossibility of God*. Amherst, NY: Prometheus Books, 351.

[13] Nicholas Everitt summarizes this view well when he writes that "indexicals necessarily have a different content from even their closest correlates. So someone who knows the truth of an indexical sentence knows something different from what is known by someone who knows only the correlates" (Nicholas Everitt (2009), *The Non-existence of God*. London: Routledge, 296).

But, as with the case of private languages, even if it is logically impossible for *S* to know the truth-value of the proposition "I am typing at this moment" (or "I am making a mess") for all *S*s not numerically identical with the individual referred to by "I," it is not clear how *S*s not numerically identical with the individual referred to by "I" *could* know what it is like not to know the truth-value of such a proposition. For *S*s not numerically identical with the individual referred to by "I" to know what it is like not to know the truth-value of a proposition involving this essential indexical, they would have to mentally entertain that proposition somehow. But, how *could* *S*s not numerically identical with the individual referred to by "I" mentally entertain the essentially indexed proposition "I am typing at this moment"? If Grim is correct, I do not see how they could. For, if they consider the sentence as is—"*I* am typing at this moment"—then they are not entertaining the same proposition since the referent of the essential indexical changes—the "I" will now refer to an *S* not numerically identical with the one typing (Rob Lovering). While if they translate the sentence to "Rob Lovering is typing at this moment"—then, once again, they are not entertaining the same proposition. Given this, and given Grim's position, I simply do not see how *S*s not numerically identical with the individual referred to by "I" could mentally entertain such essentially indexed propositions. And if they cannot mentally entertain such propositions, then I do not see how they could know what it is like not to know the truth-values of them.

So, again, what might be an example of a proposition the truth-value of which it is logically impossible for *S* to know? I, for one, cannot think of one. And, if there aren't any, then *S* cannot know what it is like not to know the truth-value of a proposition by not knowing the truth-value of a proposition it is logically impossible to know. Moreover, since *S* cannot know what it is like not to know the truth-value of a proposition by not knowing the truth-value of a proposition it is logically *possible* to know, it follows that *S* cannot know what it is like not to know the truth-value of a proposition by not knowing what it is like not to know the truth-values of propositions it is logically possible or logically impossible to know. Given this, I do not see how *S* could know what it is like not to know the truth-value of a proposition.

Objections to A2—round two

Just in case a mistake (or two) has been made above, it is worth considering a few more possibilities regarding how *S* could know what it is like not to know the truth-value of a proposition despite *S* having always known all the truth-values of all the propositions it is logically possible to know.[14]

---

[14] For a much fuller discussion of the three possibilities to be discussed here, see Torin Alter (2002), "On Two Alleged Conflicts Between Divine Attributes," *Faith and Philosophy* 19: 47–57; Yujin Nagasawa (2003), "Divine Omniscience and Experience," *Ars Disputandi* [http://www.arsdisputandi.org] 3; Linda Zagzebski (2008), "Omnisubjectivity," In Jonathan Kvanvig (ed.), *Oxford Studies in Philosophy of Religion*, Vol. 1. New York, NY: Oxford University Press, 231–48.

First, perhaps *S* could know what it is like not to know the truth-value of a proposition by way of directly perceiving the content of someone's consciousness (Joe's) who, at a time *t*, does not know the truth-value of a proposition. But, it is not at all clear that, in so doing, *S* knows what it is like not to know the truth-value of a proposition—is it that *S* knows what it is like not to know the truth-value of a proposition? Or, is it that *S* knows what it is like for *Joe* not to know the truth-value of a proposition? As with a question raised above, I see no way of settling this dispute with any confidence, if there is even a fact to the matter. Perhaps, one might argue, that *S*'s knowing what it is like for Joe not to know the truth-value of a proposition *suffices* for *S* to know what it is like not to know the truth-value of a proposition. Perhaps. Then again, perhaps not. And, once again, I see no way of settling this dispute with any confidence. But, even more problematic, this solution involves denying that *S* is essentially omniscient, as it entails that *S* did not know what it is like not to know the truth-value of a proposition prior to perceiving the content of Joe's consciousness.

Second, perhaps *S* could know what it is like not to know the truth-value of a proposition by somehow borrowing memories from Joe who, at a time *t*, did not know the truth-value of a proposition. But, as with the preceding possibility, it is not at all clear that *S* knows what it is like not to know the truth-value of a proposition rather than that *S* knows what it is like for Joe not to know the truth-value of a proposition. And, as with the preceding possibility, this possibility involves denying that *S* is essentially omniscient, as it entails that *S* did not know what it is like not to know the truth-value of a proposition prior to borrowing Joe's memories.

Third, perhaps *S* could know what it is like not to know the truth-value of a proposition by simply imagining what it is like not to know the truth-value of a proposition. But this will not do. For *S*'s imagining what it is like not to know the truth-value of a proposition to be a case of knowing what it is like not to know the truth-value of a proposition, *S* must have reasons for believing that his imagining of this experiential event is accurate.[15] And it is very difficult to see how *S* could have such reasons if he has always known the truth-value of all the propositions it is logically possible to know. Indeed, the reasons would have to be *a priori* in nature, and it is very difficult to see how one could have *a priori* reasons for thinking that one's imagining of an experiential state is accurate.

Finally, perhaps *S* could know what it is like not to know the truth-value of a proposition through testimony—Joe could tell *S* what it is like not to know the truth-value of a proposition. But, as with two previous possibilities, this possibility involves denying that *S* is essentially omniscient, as it entails that *S* did not know what it is like not to know the truth-value of a proposition prior to Joe telling *S* what it is like.

Is all experiential knowledge great-making?

Previously, I defined maximal experiential knowledge as knowledge of all that it is logically possible to know experientially. Moreover, I have argued that having experiential

---

[15] Zagzebski, "Omnisubjectivity," 239.

knowledge is a great-making quality. But *maximal* experiential knowledge—if it is truly to be maximal experiential knowledge—must encompass knowledge of what it is like to do horrible things, such as what it is like to murder someone. Given this, a question naturally arises—is all experiential knowledge great-making? Some think not. As one philosopher puts it, "Consider knowing what it is like to murder someone in cold blood, or knowing what it is like to commit a heinous sexual crime . . . None of these strikes me as great-making qualities—in fact they strike me as worse-making qualities."[16]

(Before moving on to my reply to the previous comment, it is worth pausing to note here that if knowing what it is like to murder someone is a worse-making quality, then a problem presents itself for some theistic philosophers' understanding of omniscience. Linda Zagzebski, for example, holds that omniscience includes what she calls "omnisubjectivity."[17] As she describes this property, "An omnisubjective being would know what it is like to be you, as well as what it is like to your dog, the bats in the cave, the birds, the fish, the reptiles, and each human being yet to be born."[18] If omniscience does indeed include omnisubjectivity, then God knows what it is like to be Jack the Ripper, John Wayne Gacy, and Jeffrey Dahmer, among other murderers. In turn, God knows what it is like to murder someone. If, then, omniscience does indeed include omnisubjectivity, and if knowing what it is like to murder someone is a worse-making quality, then God possesses this and many other worse-making qualities. God, then—as essentially omniscient and essentially perfectly good—is not a logically possible being. Zagzebski seems aware of and perhaps troubled by this implication, for she later writes, "I will not address the issue of whether omnisubjectivity is compatible with the other traditional divine attributes . . .")[19]

But even if knowing what it is like to murder someone is a worse-making quality, it does not follow that experiential knowledge is not great-making. All that follows is that *some* experiential knowledge is not great-making. If this is the case, then the concept of maximal experiential knowledge—when applied to God—would simply have to be further qualified. When applied to God, the concept of maximal knowledge would have to be limited not only to that which is logically possible to know experientially, but to that experiential knowledge which is great-making. (We could refer to this as "maximal great-making experiential knowledge.") Duly qualified, then, God would know what it is like to surf and to lead, but he would not know what it is like to murder someone or to commit a heinous sexual crime.

With the preceding in mind, the question for present purposes is—is knowing what it is like not to know the truth-value of a proposition the kind of experiential knowledge that is great-making or the kind of experiential knowledge that is not great-making? At first glance, one might think it is the latter. But, there is reason to think that it is the former.

To see this, let us begin with a claim that I believe most people would find uncontroversial—being good to others involves, among other things, being sympathetic

[16] Anonymous reviewer.
[17] Zagzebski, "Omnisubjectivity," 245.
[18] Ibid., 245.
[19] Ibid., 245.

to them when sympathy is called for. And, in some cases, sympathy for others is called for when the other does not know the truth-value of a proposition. For example, suppose that, through no fault of his own, Joe does not know the truth-value of the proposition "The Earth is roughly 4.5 billion years old." In this case, being good to Joe would involve having sympathy for him, among other things—it would not involve, for example, ridiculing him for being an ignoramus. Since having sympathy for another involves sharing in the other's psychological state to some extent, knowing what it is like not to know the truth-value of a proposition allows for a greater capacity for one to be good to others, for it allows for one to sympathize with them in such situations. Accordingly, knowing what it is like not to know the truth-value of a proposition is a great-making quality, for knowing what it is like not to know the truth-value of a proposition enables one to be good to those who do not know the truth-values of propositions. By knowing what it is like not to know the truth-value of a proposition, then, one is a greater being—a being more worthy of reverence and moral admiration— than one otherwise would be.[20]

Of course, even if the preceding is correct, it may be that God can have such sympathy without knowing what it is like not to know the truth-value of a proposition. So, can he? I do not see how he could. For, again, having sympathy for another involves sharing in the other's psychological state. In this case, having sympathy for someone who does not know the truth-value of a proposition involves knowing what it is like not to know the truth-value of one proposition or another. But, given A1, there is no proposition that God knows what it is like not to know its truth-value. Of course, some might think that God could know what it is like not to know the truth-value of a proposition by directly perceiving the content of someone else's consciousness who, at a time *t*, does not know the truth-value of a proposition; or by somehow borrowing memories from someone else who, at a time *t*, does not know the truth-value of a proposition; or by imagining what it is like not to know the truth-value of a proposition; or through testimony. But, as I argued in my defense of A2, each of these possibilities is either very difficult to believe or entails that God is not essentially omniscient.

An unsavory dilemma, then, presents itself—unsavory, that is, for theistic philosophers. For, either God can have such sympathy or he cannot and, either way, the logical impossibility of an essentially omniscient and essentially perfectly good

---

[20] To see this more precisely, consider Joe, who does not know the truth-value of a proposition, *p*, at a time, *t1*. At *t1*, then, Joe knows what it is like not to know the truth-value of a proposition. Now, suppose at a later time, *t2*, Joe comes to know the truth-value of *p*. In so doing, Joe acquires a greater understanding of himself, for he now knows not only what it was like for him not to know the truth-value of *p* at *t1*, but what it is like for him to know the truth-value of *p* at *t2* having previously not known the truth-value of *p*. And this greater understanding of himself allows for a greater capacity for Joe to be good to himself as well as to others. For, this greater understanding of himself enables and encourages Joe to have greater acceptance of himself with respect to what he does not know propositionally. In turn, this greater understanding serves to encourage Joe to have greater sympathy for others with respect to what they do not know propositionally. By knowing what it is like not to know the truth-value of a proposition, then, Joe is a greater being—a being more worthy of reverence and moral admiration—than he otherwise would be.

being may be inferred. If God cannot have such sympathy, then he is unable to be good to others in this way; while, if God can have such sympathy, then he knows what it is like not to know the truth-value of a proposition. God, then, cannot be essentially omniscient and essentially perfectly good.

Is there something that it is like not to know the truth-value of a proposition?

In short, yes, there is. To be sure, there isn't just one thing it is like not to know the truth-value of a proposition, just as there isn't just one thing it is like to be in love, or to surf, or to lead a platoon into battle. But there is something it is like not to know the truth-value of a proposition. What, exactly, it is like varies from proposition to proposition, but *that* there is something it is like not to know the truth-value of a proposition is, it seems to me, incontrovertible. Consider, for example, the proposition "There is intelligent life on another planet." When I reflect upon this proposition and become aware of the fact that I do not know its truth-value, a qualitative experiential shift occurs, one involving a move from a harmony of sorts to a disharmony of sorts. It isn't a dramatic shift, to be sure; it is not paralyzing, or depressing, or debilitating. But it is just that—a qualitative experiential shift. And so it is with other propositions whose truth-values I do not know, at least in many cases.

Does everyone undergo this qualitative experiential shift when they become aware of their not knowing the truth-value of a proposition? I imagine so, though I do not know for certain. But I do. Indeed, not to be overly clever, but when I reflect upon the proposition "Everyone undergoes this qualitative experiential shift when they become aware of not knowing the truth-value of a proposition" and become aware of the fact that I do not know its truth-value, I undergo this very qualitative experiential shift. And, importantly, only one instance of there being something it is like not to know the truth-value of a proposition is needed to run the argument above.

On the logical impossibility of divine omniscience—second argument

Key concepts and assumptions

The key concepts of the first argument for the logical impossibility of divine omniscience included (maximal) propositional knowledge, temporally variant and invariant propositions, (maximal) experiential knowledge, and omniscience. And, the understanding of omniscience employed was maximal propositional knowledge as well as maximal experiential knowledge. For those who still have misgivings about this understanding of omniscience, I will rely upon the restricted sense of omniscience—maximal propositional knowledge—for my second argument for the logical impossibility of divine omniscience. The use of this understanding of omniscience requires that a slight modification be made to one of my assumptions—A1. Specifically, given the restricted sense of omniscience, the second clause of A1—(ii)—must be removed. So modified, this assumption will be referred as "A1*"—necessarily, if S is essentially omniscient, then there is not a time t during S's existence at which S does not know the truth-value of a proposition. The restricted sense of omniscience has no bearing on the second assumption, A2, however, so it will remain the same—necessarily, if S knows what it is like not to know the truth-value of a proposition, then there is a time t during S's existence at which S does not know the truth-value of a proposition.

The argument

My second argument for the logical impossibility of divine omniscience takes the form of a *reductio ad absurdum*. In the following, I will first present my argument and then defend each of its premises. The argument begins as follows:

P1: Necessarily, if S is essentially omniscient, then there is not a time t during S's existence at which S does not know the truth-value of a proposition. (A1*)

P2: Necessarily, if S knows what it is like not to know the truth-value of a proposition, then there is a time t during S's existence at which S does not know the truth-value of a proposition. (A2)

P3: God is essentially omniscient. (Assumption)

C1: There is not a time t during God's existence at which God does not know the truth-value of a proposition.

C2: God does not know what it is like not to know the truth-value of a proposition.

If C2 is true, then God does not know the truth-value of the following proposition, p—"Knowing what it is like not to know the truth-value of p^* at $t1$ and then knowing what it is like to know the truth-value of p^* at $t2$ involves a qualitative experiential shift." This may be demonstrated as follows:

P4: If God does not know what it is like not to know the truth-value of a proposition, then God does not know what it is like not to know the truth-value of p^*.

C3: God does not know what it is like not to know the truth-value of p^*.

P5: If God does not know what it is like not to know the truth-value of p^*, then God does not know what it is like to shift from knowing what it is like not to know the truth-value of p^* at $t1$ to knowing what it is like to know the truth-value of p^* at $t2$.

C4: God does not know what it is like to shift from knowing what it is like not to know the truth-value of p^* at $t1$ to knowing what it is like to know the truth-value of p^* at $t2$.

P6: If God does not know what it is like to shift from knowing what it is like not to know the truth-value of p^* at $t1$ to knowing what it is like to know the truth-value of p^* at $t2$, then God does not know the truth-value of p.

C5: God does not know the truth-value of p.

Given P1–C5, a contradiction arises:

P7: If God does not know the truth-value of *p*, then there is a time *t* during God's existence at which God does not know the truth-value of a proposition.

C6: There is a time *t* during God's existence at which God does not know the truth-value of a proposition.

C7: There is a time *t* during God's existence at which God does not know the truth-value of a proposition *and* there is not a time *t* during God's existence at which God does not know the truth-value of a proposition.

C8: God is not essentially omniscient. (Reductio: P3–C7)

I will now defend each premise in turn.

Defense of P1

P1 is derived from the understanding of omniscience currently under consideration, namely, the restricted sense of omniscience.

Defense of P2

The defense of P2 has already been presented. For, P2 just is A2, and a defense of A2 was presented in the discussion of my first argument for the logical impossibility of divine omniscience. Briefly, if A2 is false, then it is possible for *S* to know what it is like not to know the truth-value of a proposition despite *S* having always known all the truth-values of all the propositions it is logically possible to know. But, as I argued above, of the possible ways in which this might be, each is either very difficult to believe or entails that God is not essentially omniscient.

Defense of P3

By "God," of course, we mean an essentially omniscient being, among other things. The *reductio* begins with this premise.

Defense of P4

Again, not knowing what it is like not to know the truth-value of a proposition is not knowing what it is like not to know the truth-value of any proposition whatsoever. If God does not know what it is like not to know the truth-value of a proposition, then God does not know what it is like not to know the truth-value of any proposition whatsoever, including this particular proposition, *p**.

Defense of P5

In order to know what it is like to *shift* from not knowing what it is like not to know the truth-value of proposition *p** at *t1* to knowing what it is like to know the truth-value of proposition p^* at $t2$, one must first know what it is like not to know the truth-value of p^*. The "must" here is both logical and psychological in nature. Logically, a shift requires at least two states of affairs—that which precedes the shift and that which succeeds the shift. In this case, the shift in question involves a shift in experiential knowledge—the preceding and succeeding states of affairs are both instances of knowing what something is like. Logically, then, the shift can occur only if one has known what it is like not to know the truth-value of p^*. And, given that knowing what something is like is psychological in nature, the shift can occur only if one has experienced a particular psychological state. So, again, the "must" here is both logical and psychological in nature.

Defense of P6

The defense of P6 hinges on the content of the proposition p. Proposition p is about what it is like to shift from knowing what it is like not to know the truth-value of p^* to knowing what it is like to know the truth-value of p^*. Knowing the truth-value of p, then, involves knowing what it is like not to know the truth-value of p^*. But, given C2, God does not know what it is like not to know the truth-value of p^*, so God does not know the truth-value of p.

Some might think that God could know what it is like not to know the truth-value of p^* and, in turn, know the truth-value of p by directly perceiving the content of someone else's consciousness who, at a time t, does not know the truth-value of p^*; or by somehow borrowing memories from someone else who, at a time t, does not know the truth-value of p^*; or by imagining what it is like not to know the truth-value of p^*; or through testimony. But, as I argued in my defense of A2, each of these possibilities is either very difficult to believe or entails that God is not essentially omniscient.

Defense of P7

If God does not know the truth-value of p, then there is a time t during God's existence at which God does not know the truth-value of a proposition, namely, the time at which God does not know the truth-value of p.

Objections to the second argument

A number of objections may be raised against my second argument for the logical impossibility of divine omniscience. One objection involves denying A2. Since I addressed this objection in the discussion of my first argument for the logical impossibility of divine omniscience, I will simply move on to a second objection.

Another objection pertains to p—knowing what it is like not to know the truth-value of p^* at $t1$ and then knowing what it is like to know the truth-value of p^* at $t2$ involves a qualitative experiential shift. Some might argue that, since p is about what it is like to undergo a certain qualitative experiential shift, God simply lacks experiential knowledge; yet, the kind of knowledge involved in the sense of omniscience currently under consideration is strictly propositional. But such a reply is misguided. To be sure, the content of p regards experiential knowledge, but p itself is a proposition. God's not knowing the truth-value of p, then, involves lacking propositional knowledge.

A final objection involves denying p—one might argue that p is not true and, thus, that my argument involves a false claim. But my argument does not require that p be true in order for it to be sound; indeed, the truth-value of p is irrelevant. What is relevant is that p is a genuine proposition and, as such, something that has a truth-value, and that God does not know the truth-value of p.

Conclusion

In this chapter, I presented two arguments for the logical impossibility of divine omniscience. With the first argument, I argued that it is not possible for God to have always possessed maximal propositional knowledge as well as maximal experiential knowledge. If God has always possessed maximal propositional knowledge, then there is a time t at which God does not possess maximal experiential knowledge. And, if God has always possessed maximal experiential knowledge, then there is a time t at which God does not possess maximal propositional knowledge. Either way, God is not—indeed, cannot be—essentially omniscient. And, even when maximal experiential knowledge is qualified—being limited not only to all that it is logically possible to know experientially, but to that experiential knowledge which is great-making—the logical impossibility of God being essentially omniscient and essentially perfectly good may be inferred.

With the second argument, I argued that the restricted sense of omniscience entails a contradiction—there is not a time t during God's existence at which God does not know the truth-value of a proposition *and* there is a time t during God's existence at which God does not know the truth-value of a proposition. Accordingly, the logical impossibility of divine omniscience is established *via reductio*.

If the preceding arguments are sound, then all three types of theistic philosopher face a significant problem, since they all believe that God—as essentially omniscient, omnipotent, and perfectly good—is a logically possible being.

Appendix: On Nonevidential Reasons for Theism

Introduction

In Chapter 1, I compared theistic philosophers to the defenders of the Alamo—just as the defenders of the Alamo were significantly outnumbered by their adversaries, so theistic philosophers are significantly outnumbered by theirs. Even so, just as the defenders of the Alamo stayed true to their convictions until the end, so it may be with the 15 percent of philosophers who accept or lean toward theism.

Do theistic philosophers have strong evidential reasons for staying so true? If they do, they are difficult to discern. As I argued above, if theistic philosophers have strong inferential and noninferential evidential reasons for believing that God exists, it is rather curious that most of their colleagues have failed to recognize, let alone accept, them.

Of course, nonevidential reasons might be at work. Indeed, nonevidential reasons might be doing more of the belief-generating work than one may have previously thought. In the following, I will provide reasons for thinking this is indeed the case. After doing so, I will argue that an important lesson may be drawn from this—one that does not reflect well on theism.

On nonevidential reasons for theism

Not all theistic philosophers embrace Pascal's or Kierkegaard's or James's or Bishop's nonevidential reasons for believing that God exists. Even so, they all likely rely upon nonevidential reasons of one sort or another for their belief that God exists, or so I shall argue. In so doing, I will put to use statements provided by contemporary theistic philosophers—including Alston, Swinburne, Plantinga, and Murray—taken from two collections of essays regarding their respective "spiritual journeys."[1]

---

[1]   See Kelly James Clark. (ed.) (1997), *Philosophers Who Believe: The Spiritual Journeys of 11 Leading Thinkers*. Downers Grove, IL: Intervarsity Press; and Thomas V. Morris. (ed.) (1996), *God and the Philosophers: The Reconciliation of Faith and Reason*. New York, NY: Oxford University Press.

Admission of nonevidential reasons

The first reason to think that theistic philosophers rely upon nonevidential reasons for their belief that God exists is rather straightforward—theistic philosophers have admitted to acquiring or retaining belief in God's existence on nonevidential grounds. Nicholas Rescher, to begin with, describes his conversion to theism as "primarily a matter of sentiment, loyalties and feelings of allegiance and kinship."[2]

Others, such as William Wainwright and C. Stephen Layman, cite Jamesian reasons for their belief that God exists. Referring to James's work on the will to believe, Wainwright writes, ". . . why have I found arguments of this kind persuasive? Because the good that religion promises seems to me so great and so splendid that we ought to pursue it with our whole heart even if that good is only possible . . ."[3] With regard to his embracing theism in particular, Wainwright declares, "The bottom line . . . is probably what James calls 'instincts,' 'divinations,' 'a sort of dumb conviction that the truth must lie in one direction rather than another,' something in us that 'whispers . . .'it must be true.'""[4]

Seconding Wainwright's approval of James's view, Layman writes of it that it

comports well with the fact that few (if any) come to faith primarily because of evidence or arguments. For example, people often come to faith because they feel that their lives are lacking in some important way and because they have the impression, based on their acquaintance with certain exemplary religious believers, that faith may be of help.[5]

Layman then describes his decision to commit fully to the Christian faith.

As for myself, after years of doubt . . . I found the halfway house of half-believing quite unsatisfying. For me personally, it was truly time to take decisive action: either reject the Christian faith and live a secular life, or else get serious about following Christ. It became clear to me, at this juncture, that both the historical figures I admired most and the persons of my acquaintance whom I most admired were men and women who had tried (or were trying) to follow Jesus Christ. This being so, why hesitate any longer? The option was momentous. I became actively involved in an Episcopal parish and plunged again into the life of the church.[6]

Still others cite Pascalian reasons for their belief that God exists. Jeff Jordan writes, ". . . there is a pragmatic reason for Christian faith . . . a 'wager argument' for Christian belief . . . The wager strikes me as persuasive—at least, I know of no good reason to think it faulty."[7]

---

[2] Nicholas Rescher, "In Matters Religion," in *Philosophers Who Believe*, 130.
[3] William J. Wainwright, "Skepticism, Romanticism and Faith," in *God and the Philosophers*, 81.
[4] Ibid., 83.
[5] C. Stephen Layman, "Faith Has Its Reasons," in *God and the Philosophers*, 92.
[6] Ibid., 92–3.
[7] Jeff Jordan, "Not in Kansas Anymore," in *God and the Philosophers*, 135.

15 percent vs. 85 percent

The second reason to think that theistic philosophers rely upon nonevidential reasons for their belief that God exists is as follows—it seems rather unlikely that the evidential reasons theistic philosophers have for believing that God exists are strong enough to be doing all the belief-generating work. It is very hard to believe, for instance, that theistic philosophers have strong evidential reasons for believing that God exists, but that 85 percent of their nontheistic colleagues have failed to appreciate the strength of those reasons. For, as I argued in Chapter 2, it is unlikely that atheistic and agnostic philosophers are intellectually or dispositionally inferior to theistic philosophers such that they do not grasp the strength of theistic philosophers' evidential reasons for believing that God exists.

Indeed, even theistic philosophers themselves concede that—at least with respect to inferential evidence—the evidence for God's existence is rather impotent. Again, as Layman writes, " . . . few (if any) come to faith primarily because of evidence or arguments."[8] Similarly, William J. Abraham writes, ". . . I had never really been a convinced believer in natural theology. The classical arguments for the existence of God were intrinsically interesting, but it had never occurred to me that they were essential to the maintenance of the rationality of religious belief."[9] In preliminary remarks to a discussion of some arguments for the Christian faith, Peter van Inwagen writes, "The arguments will almost certainly not convince anyone . . ."[10] And Alvin Plantinga, writing of his undergraduate years, expresses a view he continues to hold today, "I was still caught up in arguments about the existence of God, but they often seemed to me merely academic, of little existential concern, as if one were to argue about whether there really has been a past, for example, or whether there really were other people, as opposed to cleverly constructed robots."[11]

In addition to the preceding, there are theoretical grounds to support the view that it is unlikely that the evidential reasons theistic philosophers have for believing that God exists are strong enough to be doing all the belief-generating work. Consider Condorcet's jury theorem, a brief description of which is as follows:

> The assumptions of the simplest version of the theorem are that a group wishes to reach a decision by majority vote. One of the two outcomes of the vote is *correct*, and each voter has an independent probability p of voting for the correct decision. The theorem asks how many voters we should include in the group. The result depends on whether p is greater than or less than $1/2$: If p is greater than $1/2$ (each voter is more likely than not to vote correctly), then adding more voters increases the probability that the majority decision is correct. In the limit, the probability that the majority votes correctly approaches 1 as the number of voters increases.[12]

---

[8] Layman, "Faith Has Its Reasons," 92.
[9] William J. Abraham, "Faraway Fields Are Green," in *God and the Philosophers*, 169.
[10] Peter van Inwagen, "Quam Dilecta," in *God and the Philosophers*, 46.
[11] Alvin Plantinga, "A Christian Life Partly Lived," in *Philosophers Who Believe*, 51–2.
[12] http://en.wikipedia.org/wiki/Condorcet%27s_jury_theorem.

The decision under consideration here pertains to whether or not the evidential reasons for theism are strong. Assuming (a) that each philosopher was independently more likely than not to vote correctly and (b) that a vote for atheism or "other" is a vote that the evidential reasons for theism are *not* strong, it appears that the vote that the evidential reasons for theism are not strong is most likely to be true.

Of course, it is not clear that each philosopher *was* independently more likely than not to vote correctly. That said, I will simply note that each of these voters was a professional philosopher and if anyone was independently more likely than not to vote correctly on this matter, arguably, a professional philosopher was. As for the assumption that a vote for atheism or "other" is a vote that the evidential reasons for believing that God exists are not strong, this is all but incontrovertible, since rejecting a philosophical position almost always involves rejecting the evidential grounds (if any) on which it rests.

Belief before evidence

A third reason to think that theistic philosophers rely upon nonevidential reasons for their belief that God exists—one closely related to the four that will follow it—is that the vast majority of them believed or were raised to believe in God's existence well before seriously and philosophically assessing the evidence for and against God's existence.[13] To wit—in the aforementioned collections of essays regarding the spiritual journeys of contemporary theistic philosophers, 93 percent of the philosophers who addressed their upbringing (26 out of the 28) believed or were raised to believe in God's existence well before seriously and philosophically assessing the evidence for and against God's existence. Hence, claims such as:

- "As far back as my memory stretches I recall having thought in Christian terms." (Richard Swinburne)
- "Two things have dominated my life from the beginning: a love of learning and a desire for God." (Marilyn McCord Adams)
- ". . . I have no memory of a time when I did not believe." (Jeff Jordan)
- ". . . for nearly my entire life I have been convinced of the *truth* of Christianity." (Alvin Plantinga)[14]

And that the vast majority of these theistic philosophers believed or were raised to believe in God's existence well before seriously and philosophically assessing the

---

[13] One exception is C. S. Lewis, who reportedly came to believe in God's existence *after* examining the evidence as (for all intents and purposes) a professional philosopher. But the exceptions are just that, exceptions. Indeed, it is seemingly *because* they are exceptional in this way that such conversions are deemed remarkable—so remarkable that, in Lewis's case (for example), one is hard pressed to find a biography of Lewis that does not emphasize if not celebrate how he came to believe in God's existence.

[14] See Richard Swinburne, "The Vocation of a Natural Theologian," in *Philosophers Who Believe*, 179; Marilyn McCord Adams, "Love of Learning, Reality of God," in *God and the Philosophers*, 137; Jordan, "Not in Kansas Anymore," 129; Plantinga, "A Christian Life Partly Lived," 69.

evidence for and against God's existence indicates that nonevidential reasons are at work. As Layman writes,

> . . . in the typical case, I think there are potent nonevidential causes of religious belief. For example, many Christians were brought up in the faith, and this sort of upbringing inevitably involves some psychological conditioning.[15]

And so it is, *mutatis mutandis*, with those theistic philosophers who were brought up in non-Christian theistic faiths, such as Judaism and Islam.

Granted, it is not clear just how strong an influence nonevidential reasons such as psychological conditioning have in these cases. But it is worth noting that, generally speaking, people are unlikely to abandon the religious beliefs in which they were raised. According to a recent survey by the Pew Forum on Religion and Public Life—involving interviews with more than 35,000 Americans aged 18 and over— only 28 percent of them "left the faith in which they were raised in favor of another religion—or no religion at all."[16] Nearly three in four, then, remained in the faith in which they were raised; and an even greater percentage remained theists, as some of those who left the faith in which they were raised went from one theistic faith to another (e.g., from Christianity to Islam, or vice versa).

Moreover, when these theistic philosophers eventually got around to seriously and philosophically assessing the evidence for and against God's existence, the vast majority of them did so under the tutelage of theistic professors at explicitly theistic institutions. These institutions—some of which are cited by multiple theistic philosophers— include Calvin College, Wheaton College, Westmont College, Circleville Bible College, Houghton College, Whitworth College (now Whitworth University), Asbury Theological Seminary, Fuller Theological Seminary, Princeton Theological Seminary, and Yale Divinity School. Lest there be any confusion as to where the intellectual and philosophical loyalties of these institutions and their faculty lie, consider portions of their mission statements and/or mottos:

- Calvin College is a comprehensive liberal arts college in the Reformed tradition of historic Christianity . . . We pledge fidelity to Jesus Christ, offering our hearts and lives to do God's work in God's world.[17]
- Wheaton College exists to help build the church and improve society worldwide by promoting the development of whole and effective Christians through excellence in programs of Christian higher education . . . This mission expresses our commitment to do all things – "For Christ and His Kingdom."[18]
- Westmont College is an undergraduate, residential, Christian, liberal arts community serving God's kingdom by cultivating thoughtful scholars, grateful

---

[15] Layman, "Faith Has Its Reasons," 97.
[16] http://religions.pewforum.org/reports.
[17] https://www.calvin.edu/about/mission.html.
[18] http://www.wheaton.edu/About-Wheaton/Mission.

servants and faithful leaders for global engagement with the academy, church and
world . . . The motto, *Christus Primatum Tenens,* Christ holding first place, comes
from Colossians 1:18 – "That in all things He might have the preeminence."[19]

* Houghton College provides an academically challenging, Christ-centered
  education in the liberal arts and sciences to students from diverse traditions and
  economic backgrounds and equips them to lead and labor as scholar-servants in a
  changing world.[20]
* Whitworth's mission is to provide its diverse student body an education of
  mind and heart, equipping its graduates to honor God, follow Christ, and serve
  humanity. This mission is carried out by a community of Christian scholars
  committed to excellent teaching and to the integration of faith and learning.[21]
* In all of our activities, including instruction, nurture, worship, service, research,
  and publication, Fuller Theological Seminary strives for excellence in the service of
  Jesus Christ, under the guidance and power of the Holy Spirit, to the glory of the
  Father.[22]
* Princeton Theological Seminary prepares women and men to serve Jesus Christ
  in ministries marked by faith, integrity, scholarship, competence, compassion,
  and joy, equipping them for leadership worldwide in congregations and the larger
  church, in classrooms and the academy, and in the public arena.[23]

Needless to say, when a young theist begins seriously and philosophically assessing
the evidence for and against God's existence under the tutelage of theistic professors
at explicitly theistic institutions with explicit intellectual commitments to theism,
it is unlikely that he or she will be encouraged to take anti-theistic arguments *too*
seriously—at least, to take them as seriously as they are encouraged to take pro-theistic
arguments—much less that he or she will do so.

Confirmation bias

A fourth reason to think that theistic philosophers rely upon nonevidential reasons for
their belief that God exists is closely related to the previous reason. The reluctance to give
up the religious beliefs of one's upbringing is likely due in part to what psychologists call
"confirmation bias." Confirmation bias is "a tendency for people to favor information
that confirms their preconceptions or hypotheses regardless of whether the information
is true."[24] And, according to a recent analysis of psychological studies involving nearly
8,000 participants, "people are twice as likely to seek information that confirms what
they already believe as they are to consider evidence that would challenge those

---

19 http://www.westmont.edu/_offices/president/statement_of_faith.html.
20 http://www.houghton.edu/about-us/.
21 http://www.whitworth.edu/GeneralInformation/Mission.htm.
22 http://www.fuller.edu/about-fuller/mission-and-history/mission-beyond-the-mission.aspx.
23 http://www.ptsem.edu/index.aspx?menu1_id=2030&menu2_id=2031&id=1237.
24 http://en.wikipedia.org/wiki/Confirmation_bias.

beliefs."[25] Obviously, confirmation bias is not peculiar to theistic philosophers. But, it may be especially acute in their case, at least with respect to some of them. As Brian Leftow writes:

> Christian commitment . . . is not just abstractly intellectual. It is passionate. It involves hopes, ideals, self-discipline, and personal sacrifice. Passions can tempt one to intellectual dishonesty. Further, the more hope and effort one invests in a religious belief, the more it would hurt to find that belief false, and the more foolish one would feel. So depth of Christian commitment can also tempt one to intellectual dishonesty—for example, weighing anti-Christian arguments unfairly.[26]

Leftow all but explicitly acknowledges here that, with respect to God's existence (among other things), confirmation bias may be especially acute among some theistic philosophers. Indeed, his comments indicate that some theistic philosophers may be especially vulnerable to a related bias, one that is known as "sunk-cost bias"—the tendency to believe in something because of the cost sunk into that belief.[27]

Similarly, Jeff Jordan writes,

> . . . faithful religious belief, especially a mature faithful belief, involves a deep commitment to the object of faith, a commitment that is nearly unreserved and unconditional. So, for the religious believer, there are certain beliefs or certain claims that are not just tentatively held but are decisively thought to be true. These religious beliefs are, except perhaps in the most theoretical sense, beyond the pale of revision. To a degree, faith is an attitude that disregards any need of any further inquiry into the legitimacy of that faith. Indeed, to grow in the faith is to grow in one's firmness of hold on the beliefs of the faith.[28]

Like Leftow, Jordan all but explicitly acknowledges here that, with respect to God's existence (again, among other things), confirmation bias may be especially acute among some theistic philosophers.

The priority of religion

Speaking of confirmation bias, a fifth reason to think that theistic philosophers rely upon nonevidential reasons for their belief that God exists has to do with the advice Alvin Plantinga gives them in his "Advice to Christian Philosophers." (Though directed

---

[25] http://online.wsj.com/article/SB10001424052748703811604574533680037778184.html; see also, Raymond S. Nickerson (1998), "Confirmation Bias: A Ubiquitous Phenomenon in Many Guises," in *Review of General Psychology* 2(2): 175–220; Charles Lord, Lee Ross, and Mark Lepper (1979), "Biased Assimilation and Attitude Polarization: The Effects of Prior Theories on Subsequently Considered Evidence," in *Journal of Personality and Social Psychology* 37(11): 2098–109.

[26] Brian Leftow, "From Jerusalem to Athens," in *God and the Philosophers*, 199.

[27] Michael Shermer (2011), *The Believing Brain*. New York, NY: Times Books, 265ff.

[28] Jordan, 130–1.

at Christian philosophers, his advice is "relevant to all philosophers who believe in God, whether Christian, Jewish or Moslem.")[29] The advice is as follows:

[W]e who are Christians and propose to be philosophers must not rest content with being philosophers who happen, incidentally, to be Christians; we must strive to be Christian philosophers. We must therefore pursue our projects with integrity, independence, and Christian boldness.[30]

And, in another context, Plantinga advises that

Christian philosophers should *explicitly* and *self-consciously* think of themselves as belonging to the Christian community (and the community of Christian intellectuals); perhaps they should think of themselves *primarily* or *first of all* as members of the Christian community, and only secondarily as members of, say, the philosophical community at large, or the contemporary academic community. Our first responsibility is to the Lord and to the Christian community, not first of all to the philosophical community at large . . .[31]

On virtually any reading of these statements, Plantinga's advice to theistic philosophers seems to be that, at least as a general rule, when it comes to deciding between their theistic beliefs and beliefs that conflict with them, their pre- if not post-critical allegiance should be to their theistic beliefs. (Plantinga even teaches young theists how to do this in a course titled "How to Be a Christian Philosopher.")[32]

Granted, it is unclear exactly how many theistic philosophers agree with Plantinga's advice, let alone behave accordingly. But at least one philosopher attributes what he deems to be a revival of Christian philosophy to Plantinga's advice, writing, "The philosophical and Christian boldness of Plantinga's address engendered an immense flowering of Christian philosophy in the subsequent decade."[33] And other theistic philosophers have subsequently given similar advice in print. Laura L. Garcia, for example, writes that ". . . one is not first committed to the academic life and only secondarily to Christianity; rather, one is first a believer, and the question is whether the scholarly profession fits with that more fundamental commitment."[34]

Faith seeking understanding

A sixth reason to think that theistic philosophers rely upon nonevidential reasons for their belief that God exists pertains to their view of the role of philosophy with respect to their religious beliefs. Many theistic philosophers hold that the role of philosophy with respect to their religious beliefs is that of a handmaiden. As William Alston puts it:

[29] Alvin Plantinga, "Advice to Christian Philosophers," http://www.leaderu.com/truth/1truth10.html.
[30] Ibid., http://www.leaderu.com/truth/1truth10.html.
[31] Plantinga, "A Christian Life Partly Lived," 78.
[32] http://www.calvin.edu/news/archive/a-serious-love
[33] Kelly James Clark, "Introduction," in *Philosophers Who Believe*, 10.
[34] Laura L. Garcia, "Philosophy and Faith," in *God and the Philosophers*, 173.

. . . philosophical thinking can play a crucial role in coming to a deeper understanding of the faith. "Faith seeking understanding" is a motto by which I try to live. Philosophy always has been, and continues to be, a primary tool in the ongoing attempt to gain a more penetrating grasp of the import of the basic articles of faith: the nature of God, creation, sin, the Incarnation, the atonement, the work of the Spirit, and so on. But when faith is seeking understanding, the faith is already there, and philosophy comes on the scene too late to produce it . . . The general upshot of all this is that although philosophical reasoning has very important roles to play in the religious life, producing faith where it had been absent is not one of them.[35]

Similarly, Abraham writes,

Philosophy has a more modest role in the life of faith. It can clear away obstacles, clarify crucial concepts and options, lay bare the process of relevant justification, make manifest hidden assumptions, bring to light unforeseen consequences of belief, open up to view contradictions and paradoxes, and the like. These are intrinsically important to creatures endowed with reason, and they have their own place in the fostering of the intellectual love of our great God and Savior.[36]

And Leftow writes, "For me, philosophy is an effort to fill in the details and resolve difficulties my beliefs face. I think out my faith, and I think out of my faith."[37]

A lesson learned

It is clear, then, that theistic philosophers rely upon nonevidential reasons for their belief that God exists. But, so what? What lessons may be drawn from this? By itself, not many—at least, not many of philosophical import. But, when this fact is combined with two other facts:

i. that the evidential reasons for theism are found by most philosophers to be wanting (as indicated by the aforementioned survey), and,
ii. that many theistic philosophers claim to have embraced or retained their belief that God exists on the basis of private, noninferential evidence (to be discussed immediately hereafter),

a lesson may be drawn, and it is one that does not reflect well on theism. To see this, consider the following.

In both of the collections of essays mentioned previously, every one of the theistic philosophers who claims evidence played an important role in his or her embracing or

---

[35] William Alston, "A Philosopher's Way Back," in *God and the Philosophers*, 27.
[36] Abraham, 172.
[37] Leftow, 197. See also Merold Westphal, "Faith Seeking Understanding," in *God and the Philosophers*, 216.

retaining their belief in God's existence also claims that the evidence was private and noninferential in nature. Here are some examples:

- "... it seemed to me as though I felt God's presence in the beauty of these natural wonders, that I was standing before Him, their maker and their life ... from the perspective of the believer, coming to God often seems more like an encounter than like solving a math problem ... In the end, I can only say that I believe I know the voice of God when he speaks to me, and that this is where He has led me. I think that in any such move from unbelief to faith, intellectual considerations will take one only so far. Ultimately, it is always a matter of hearing the voice of God as addressed to oneself, as calling one's own name, and of choosing to listen and obey." (Laura L. Garcia)[38]
- "I was sitting in the library reading Alasdair McIntyre's early (and bad) essay 'Visions' (which ridicules the evidential value of religious experience) when my if's, and's, and but's about God ran out. None of my questions had been answered, but I was filled with an overpowering sense of the real presence of God right there in the library. Nor was it a fleeting presence. God remained a given in experience, just as He had been in my childhood, along with sunshine, green grass, and the vast Midwestern skies. I was overjoyed." (Marilyn McCord Adams)[39]
- "... I began to feel God was calling me. Once we are disarmed of the intellectual barriers that we use to shield ourselves from God, the call of God becomes awfully clear ... This 'calling' is surely mysterious to those who are not Christians—it was to me before my own conversion. There was no voice calling 'Take up, read' but the subtle call is well expressed as the 'still, small voice.' " (Michael J. Murray)[40]
- "The two events that resolved these doubts and ambivalences for me occurred during my second semester. One gloomy evening ... I was returning from dinner, walking past Widenar Library to my fifth-floor room in Thayer Middle ... It was dark, windy, raining, nasty. But suddenly it was as if the heavens opened; I heard, so it seemed, music of overwhelming power and grandeur and sweetness; there was light of unimaginable splendor and beauty; it seemed I could see into heaven itself; and I suddenly saw or perhaps felt with great clarity and persuasion and conviction that the Lord was really there and was all I had thought. The effects of this experience lingered for a long time; I was still caught up in arguments about the existence of God, but they often seemed to me merely academic, of little existential concern." (Alvin Plantinga)[41]

And, when combined with two previously mentioned facts—that the evidential reasons for theism are found by most philosophers to be wanting and that nonevidential reasons are clearly at work—this fact suggests the following lesson—that we be very skeptical of theism. Perhaps the best way to demonstrate this is to shift gears for a moment and view

---

[38] Garcia, 174–5 and 181.
[39] Adams, 145.
[40] Michael J. Murray, "Seek and You Will Find," in *God and the Philosophers*, 74.
[41] Plantinga, "A Christian Life Partly Lived," 51–2.

all that has been discussed in this appendix through the lens of a nontheistic religion, such as Raëlism.

Suppose all of the following were true of the leading philosophical defenders of Raëlism:

- that many of them admit to embracing Raëlism on the basis of nonevidential reasons, with one defender saying, "The good that Raëlism promises seems to me so great and so splendid that we ought to pursue it with our whole heart even if that good is only possible";
- that 85 percent of their philosophical counterparts reject Raëlism;
- that the vast majority of them believed or were raised to believe in Raëlism well before seriously and philosophically assessing the evidence for and against Raëlism;
- that when they eventually got around to seriously and philosophically assessing the evidence for and against Raëlism, the vast majority of them did so under the tutelage of Raëlian professors at explicitly Raëlian institutions—institutions whose missions statements included statements such as:

  - We pledge fidelity to our extraterrestrial creators, offering our hearts and lives to do their work in their world.
  - We exist to help build the church and improve society worldwide by promoting the development of whole and effective Raëlians through excellence in programs of Raëlian higher education. This mission expresses our commitment to do all things – "For our extraterrestrial creators and their kingdom."
  - We are an undergraduate, residential, Raëlian, liberal arts community serving our extraterrestrial creators' kingdom by cultivating thoughtful scholars, grateful servants and faithful leaders for global engagement with the academy, church and world.

- that their Raëlian commitment is not just abstractly intellectual. It is passionate, involving hopes, ideals, self-discipline, and personal sacrifice. And, their passions can tempt them to intellectual dishonesty. Further, the more hope and effort they invest in Raëlism, the more it would hurt to find it false, and the more foolish they would feel. So depth of Raëlian commitment also tempts them to intellectual dishonesty—for example, weighing anti-Raëlian arguments unfairly;
- that they accept the following advice from one of their own—that those who are Raëlians and propose to be philosophers must not rest content with being philosophers who happen, incidentally, to be Raëlians; they must strive to be Raëlian philosophers. They must therefore pursue their projects with integrity, independence, and Raëlian boldness. (This leading philosophical defender of Raëlism even teaches young Raëlians how to do this in a course titled "How to Be a Raëlian Philosopher.");
- that they adopt a "faith seeking understanding" approach to philosophy—the role of philosophy with respect to their Raëlian beliefs is that of a handmaiden, with one defender saying, "The general upshot is that although philosophical reasoning

has very important roles to play in Raëlism, producing faith where it had been absent is not one of them"; and

- that the kind of evidence that led them to embrace or retain Raëlism is typically private, noninferential evidence. As some of them put it:

  - "This 'calling' is surely mysterious to those who are not Raëlians—it was to me before my own conversion. There was no voice calling 'Take up, read' but the subtle call is well expressed as the 'still, small voice.'"
  - "I was sitting in the library reading Alasdair McIntyre's early (and bad) essay 'Visions' (which ridicules the evidential value of religious experience) when my if's, and's, and but's about my extraterrestrial creators ran out. None of my questions had been answered, but I was filled with an overpowering sense of the real presence of my extraterrestrial creators right there in the library. Nor was it a fleeting presence. My extraterrestrial creators remained a given in experience, just as they had been in my childhood, along with sunshine, green grass, and the vast Midwestern skies. I was overjoyed."
  - "It seemed to me as though I felt my extraterrestrial creators' presence in the beauty of these natural wonders, that I was standing before my extraterrestrial creators . . . from the perspective of the believer, coming to our extraterrestrial creators often seems more like an encounter than like solving a math problem . . . In the end, I can only say that I believe I know the voices of our extraterrestrial creators when they speak to me, and that this is where they have led me . . . Ultimately, it is always a matter of hearing the voices of our extraterrestrial creators as addressed to oneself, as calling one's own name, and of choosing to listen and obey."

I have no doubt that the vast majority of us—philosophers and non-philosophers alike—would be *very* skeptical of Raëlism if all of this were true of its leading philosophical defenders. Shouldn't we be very skeptical of theism, then, since this is true of its leading philosophical defenders? To be sure, theism is statistically more popular than Raëlism. But, in and of itself, this is no reason to think that we should be less skeptical of it. So, again, shouldn't we be very skeptical of theism since this is true of its leading philosophical defenders? Given what I have covered here as well as what has been argued in many other excellent critiques of theism, I am inclined to think that we should.[42]

---

[42] For excellent critiques of theism, see Nicholas Everitt (2004), *The Non-existence of God*. New York, NY: Routledge; Michael Martin (1990), *Atheism: A Philosophical Justification*. Philadelphia: Temple University Press; J. L. Mackie (1983), *The Miracle of Theism*. Oxford: Oxford University Press; Michael Martin and Ricki Monnier (eds) (2006), *The Improbability of God*. Amherst, NY: Prometheus Books; Michael Martin and Ricki Monnier (eds) (2003), *The Impossibility of God*. Amherst, NY: Prometheus Books; J. L. Schellenberg (2007), *The Wisdom to Doubt*. Ithaca, NY: Cornell University Press; J. L. Schellenberg (1993), *Divine Hiddenness and Human Reason*. Ithaca, NY: Cornell University Press.

Bibliography

Abraham, William J. (1994) "Faraway Fields Are Green." In Thomas V. Morris (ed.), *God and the Philosophers: The Reconciliation of Faith and Reason*. New York, NY: Oxford University Press, pp. 162–72.

Adams, Marilyn McCord. (1994) "Love of Learning, Reality of God." In Thomas V. Morris (ed.), *God and the Philosophers: The Reconciliation of Faith and Reason*. New York, NY: Oxford University Press, pp. 137–61.

Adler, Jonathan. (2006) *Belief's Own Ethics*. Cambridge, MA: MIT Press.

Alston, William P. (1983) "Christian Experience and Christian Belief." In Alvin Plantinga and Nicholas Wolterstorff (eds), *Faith and Rationality: Reason and Belief in God*. Notre Dame, IN: University of Notre Dame Press, pp. 103–34.

—. (1991) *Perceiving God: The Epistemology of Religious Experience*. Ithaca, NY: Cornell University Press.

—. (1994) "A Philosopher's Way Back." In Thomas V. Morris (ed.), *God and the Philosophers: The Reconciliation of Faith and Reason*. New York, NY: Oxford University Press, pp. 9–30.

—. (2008) "Religious Experience and Religious Belief." In Louis P. Pojman and Michael Rea (eds), *Philosophy of Religion: An Anthology*, 5th edition. Belmont, CA: Thomson Wadsworth, pp. 136–42.

Alter, Torin. (2002) "On Two Alleged Conflicts Between Divine Attributes." *Faith and Philosophy* 19: 47–57.

Antony, Louise M. (ed.) (2007) *Philosophers Without Gods: Meditations on Atheism and the Secular Life*. Oxford: Oxford University Press.

Aquinas, Thomas. (1996) "Faith, Analogy, and Five Proofs for God." In Ed. L. Miller (ed.), *Believing in God: Readings on Faith and Reason*. Upper Saddle River, NJ: Prentice Hall, pp. 27–38.

Becker, Lawrence C. and Charlotte B. Becker. (eds) (2003) *A History of Western Ethics*, 2nd edition. New York, NY: Routledge.

Behe, Michael. (1998) *Darwin's Black Box: The Biochemical Challenge to Evolution*. New York, NY: Free Press.

Bishop, John. (2007) *Believing By Faith: An Essay in the Epistemology and Ethics of Religious Belief*. Oxford: Clarendon Press.

Clack, Beverley and Brian Clack. (2008) *The Philosophy of Religion: A Critical Introduction*, 2nd edition. Cambridge: Polity.

Clark, Kelly James. (ed.) (1997) *Philosophers Who Believe: The Spiritual Journeys of 11 Leading Thinkers*. Downers Grove, IL: Intervarsity Press.

Clifford, William K. (2008) "The Ethics of Belief." In Louis P. Pojman and Michael Rea (eds), *Philosophy of Religion: An Anthology*, 5th edition. Belmont, CA: Thomson Wadsworth, pp. 366–9.

Collins, Robin. (2008) "A Scientific Argument for the Existence of God." In Louis P. Pojman and Michael Rea (eds), *Philosophy of Religion: An Anthology*, 5th edition. Belmont, CA: Thomson Wadsworth, pp. 74–91.

Craig, William Lane. (1992) "The Origin and Creation of the Universe: A Response to Adolf Grünbaum." *British Journal for the Philosophy of Science* 43: 233–40.

—. (2010) "The Kalām Cosmological Argument." In Michael Peterson, William Hasker, Bruce Reichenbach and David Basinger (eds),, *Philosophy of Religion: Selected Readings*, 4th edition. New York, NY: Oxford University Press, pp. 197–204.

Craig, William Lane and James P. Moreland. (2008) "The Kalām Cosmological Argument." In Louis P. Pojman and Michael Rea (eds), *Philosophy of Religion: An Anthology*, 5th edition. Belmont, CA: Thomson Wadsworth, pp. 33–44.

Creel, Richard E. (2003) "Faith as Imperfect Knowledge." In Elizabeth S. Radcliffe and Carol J. White (eds), *Faith in Theory and Practice*. Peru, IL: Open Court Publishing, pp. 67–73.

Davis, Stephen T. (1978) *Faith, Skepticism, and Evidence*. Cranbury, NJ: Associated University Presses.

Dawkins, Richard. (2008) "Science Versus Religion." In Louis P. Pojman and Michael Rea (eds), *Philosophy of Religion: An Anthology*, 5th edition. Belmont, CA: Thomson Wadsworth, pp. 426–9.

Dennett, Daniel. (2006) *Breaking the Spell: Religion as Natural Phenomenon*. New York, NY: Penguin Books.

Dennett, Daniel and Alvin Plantinga. (2011) *Science and Religion: Are They Compatible?* New York, NY: Oxford University Press.

Dretske, Fred. (2005) "Is Knowledge Closed Under Known Entailment? The Case Against Closure." In Matthias Steup and Ernest Sosa (eds), *Contemporary Debates in Epistemology*. Oxford: Blackwell, pp. 13–25.

Everitt, Nicholas. (2004) *The Non-existence of God*. New York, NY: Routledge.

—. (2010) "The Divine Attributes." *Philosophy Compass* 5: 78–90.

Freud, Sigmund. (1989) *The Future of an Illusion*, Standard Edition. New York, NY: W. W. Norton & Company.

Gale, Richard M. (1993) *On the Nature and Existence of God*. Cambridge: Cambridge University Press.

—. (2007) *On the Philosophy of Religion*. Belmont, CA: Thomson Wadsworth.

Garcia, Laura L. (1994) "Philosophy and Faith." In Thomas V. Morris (ed.), *God and the Philosophers: The Reconciliation of Faith and Reason*. New York, NY: Oxford University Press, pp. 173–81.

Grim, Patrick. (2003) "Against Omniscience: The Case from Essential Indexicals." In Michael Martin and Ricki Monnier (eds), *The Impossibility of God*. Amherst, NY: Prometheus Books, pp. 349–80.

Harris, Sam. (2004) *The End of Faith*. New York, NY: W. W. Norton and Company.

Helm, Paul. (1994) *Belief Policies*. Cambridge: Cambridge University Press.

—. (1997) *Faith & Understanding*. Grand Rapids, MI: Wm. B. Eerdmans Publishing Co.

—. (2004) "God Does Not Take Risks." In Michael L. Peterson and Raymond J. Vanarragon (eds), *Contemporary Debates in Philosophy of Religion*. New York, NY: Blackwell Publishing, pp. 228–38.

Hick, John H. (1966) *Evil and the Love of God*. New York, NY: Harper and Row.

Hoffman, Joshua and Gary S. Rosenkrantz. (2002) *The Divine Attributes*. New York, NY: Blackwell Publishing.

Howard-Snyder, Daniel. (1998) "God, Evil, and Suffering." In Michael J. Murray (ed.), *Reason for the Hope Within*. Grand Rapids, MI: Wm. B. Eerdmans Publishing Co, pp. 76–115.

Hume, David. (2008) "Against Miracles." In Louis P. Pojman and Michael Rea (eds), *Philosophy of Religion: An Anthology*, 5th edition. Belmont, CA: Thomson Wadsworth, pp. 276–84.

—. (2009) "The Argument to Design and the Problem of Evil." In Steven M. Cahn (ed.), *Exploring Philosophy of Religion: An Introductory Anthology*. New York, NY: Oxford University Press, pp. 78–96.

Hurley, Patrick. (2011) *A Concise Introduction to Logic*, 11th edition. Belmont, CA: Wadsworth Publishing.

Jordan, Jeff. (1994) "Not in Kansas Anymore." In Thomas V. Morris (ed.), *God and the Philosophers: The Reconciliation of Faith and Reason*. New York, NY: Oxford University Press, pp. 128–36.

Kenny, Anthony. (1979) *The God of the Philosophers*. Oxford: Oxford University Press.

—. (1989) *The Metaphysics of the Mind*. Oxford: Oxford University Press.

Kierkegaard, Søren. (1941) *Concluding Unscientific Postscript*, trans. David E. Swenson and Walter Lowrie. Princeton, NJ: Princeton University Press.

Kornblith, Hilary. (1986) "Naturalizing Rationality." In Newton Garver and Peter H. Hare (eds), *Naturalism and Rationality*. Buffalo, NY: Prometheus Books, pp. 115–33.

Kretzmann, Norman. (1966) "Omniscience and Immutability." *Journal of Philosophy* 63: 409–21.

Layman, C. Stephen. (1994) "Faith Has Its Reasons." In Thomas V. Morris (ed.), *God and the Philosophers: The Reconciliation of Faith and Reason*. New York, NY: Oxford University Press, pp. 88–101.

Leftow, Brian. (1994) "From Jerusalem to Athens." In Thomas V. Morris (ed.), *God and the Philosophers: The Reconciliation of Faith and Reason*. New York, NY: Oxford University Press.

Lewis, Clive S. (2001) *Mere Christianity*. San Francisco: HarperSanFrancisco.

Lewis, David. (2009) "Divine Evil." In Kevin Timpe (ed.), *Arguing About Religion*. New York, NY: Routledge, pp. 472–81.

Lord, Charles, Lee Ross, and Mark Lepper. (1979) "Biased Assimilation and Attitude Polarization: The Effects of Prior Theories on Subsequently Considered Evidence." *Journal of Personality and Social Psychology* 37(11): 2098–109.

MacIntyre, Alasdair. (1998) *A Short History of Ethics: A History of Moral Philosophy from the Homeric Age to the Twentieth Century*. New York, NY: Routledge.

Mackie, John L. (2008) "Evil and Omnipotence." In Louis P. Pojman and Michael Rea (eds), *Philosophy of Religion: An Anthology*, 5th edition. Belmont, CA: Thomson Wadsworth, pp. 173–80.

Martin, Michael. (1990) *Atheism: A Philosophical Justification*. Philadelphia: Temple University Press.

—. (ed.) (2007) *The Cambridge Companion to Atheism*. Cambridge: Cambridge University Press.

Martin, Michael and Ricki Monnier. (eds) (2003) *The Impossibility of God*. Amherst, NY: Prometheus Books.

—. (eds) (2006) *The Improbability of God*. Amherst, NY: Prometheus Books.

Mavrodes, George. (1983) "Jerusalem and Athens Revisited." In Alvin Plantinga and Nicholas Wolterstorff (eds), *Faith and Rationality: Reason and Belief in God*. Notre Dame, IN: University of Notre Dame Press, pp. 192–218.

—. (1999) "Omniscience." In Philip L. Quinn and Charles Taliaferro (eds), *A Companion to Philosophy of Religion*. Malden, MA: Wiley-Blackwell Publishing, pp. 236–42.

McCord Adams, Marilyn. (1994) "Love of Learning, Reality of God." In Thomas V. Morris (ed.), *God and the Philosophers: The Reconciliation of Faith and Reason*. New York, NY: Oxford University Press, pp. 137–61.

Mill, John Stuart. (1963) *The Collected Works of John Stuart Mill*, Vol. 9, edited by J. M. Robson. Toronto: University of Toronto Press.

Mion, Giovanni. (2012) "God, Ignorance, and Existence." In *International Journal for Philosophy of Religion* 72(2): 85–8.

Morris, Thomas V. (ed.) (1996) *God and the Philosophers: The Reconciliation of Faith and Reason*. New York, NY: Oxford University Press.

—. (2003) "Omnipotence and Omniscience." In Charles Taliaferro and Paul J. Griffiths (eds), *Philosophy of Religion: An Anthology*. Malden, MA: Blackwell Publishing, pp. 58–72.

Morriston, Wes. (2000) "What Is So Good About Moral Freedom?" *The Philosophical Quarterly* 50(200): 344–58.

—. (2002) "A Critique of the Kalām Cosmological Argument." In Ray Martin and Christopher Bernard (eds), *God Matters: Readings in the Philosophy of Religion*. New York, NY: Longman Press, pp. 95–108.

Moser, Paul K. (2002) "Cognitive Idolatry and Divine Hiding." In Daniel Howard-Snyder and Paul K. Moser (eds), *Divine Hiddenness: New Essays*. New York, NY: Cambridge University Press, pp. 120–48.

—. (2004) "Divine Hiddenness Does Not Justify Atheism." In Michael L. Peterson and Raymond J. Vanarragon (eds), *Contemporary Debates in Philosophy of Religion*. Malden, MA: Blackwell Publishing, pp. 42–53.

Murray, Michael J. (1993) "Coercion and the Hiddenness of God." *American Philosophical Quarterly* 30(1): 27–38.

—. (1994) "Seek and You Will Find." In Thomas V. Morris (ed.), *God and the Philosophers: The Reconciliation of Faith and Reason*. New York, NY: Oxford University Press, pp. 61–76.

—. (2002) "Deus Absconditus." In Daniel Howard-Snyder and Paul K. Moser (eds), *Divine Hiddenness: New Essays*. Cambridge: Cambridge University Press, pp. 62–82.

Nagasawa, Yujin. (2003) "Divine Omniscience and Experience." *Ars Disputandi* [http://www.arsdisputandi.org] 3.

Nickerson, Raymond S. (1998) "Confirmation Bias: A Ubiquitous Phenomenon in Many Guises." *Review of General Psychology* 2(2): 175–220.

Oppy, Graham. (2006) *Arguing About Gods*. Cambridge: Cambridge University Press.

—. Review of *Reason for the Hope Within*. http://www.infidels.org/library/modern/graham_oppy/hope-within.html.

Paley, William. (2009) "The Argument to Design." In Steven M. Cahn (ed.), *Exploring Philosophy of Religion: An Introductory Anthology*. New York, NY: Oxford University Press, pp. 74–7.

Pascal, Blaise. (2009) "The Wager." In Steven M. Cahn (ed.), *Exploring Philosophy of Religion: An Introductory Anthology*. New York, NY: Oxford University Press, pp. 191–2.

Plantinga, Alvin. (1974) *The Nature of Necessity*. Oxford: Clarendon Press.

—. (1983) "Reason and Belief in God." In Alvin Plantinga and Nicholas Wolterstorff (eds), *Faith and Rationality: Reason and Belief in God*. Notre Dame, IN: University of Notre Dame Press, pp. 16–93.

—. (1991) *God, Freedom, and Evil.* Grand Rapids, MI: Wm. B. Eerdmans Publishing Co.

—. (1993a) "A Christian Life Partly Lived." In Kelly James Clark (ed.), *Philosophers Who Believe: The Spiritual Journeys of 11 Leading Thinkers.* Downers Grove, IL: InterVarsity Press, pp. 45–82.

—. (1993b) *Warrant: The Current Debate.* New York, NY: Oxford University Press.

—. (2000) *Warranted Christian Belief.* New York, NY: Oxford University Press.

Plantinga, Alvin and Michael Tooley. (2008) *Knowledge of God.* Malden, MA: Blackwell Publishing.

Pojman, Louis P. and Michael Rea. (2008) "Part 1." In Louis P. Pojman and Michael Rea (eds), *Philosophy of Religion: An Anthology,* 5th edition. Belmont, CA: Thomson Wadsworth, pp. 1–2.

Priest, Graham. (2001) *An Introduction to Non-Classical Logic.* Cambridge: Cambridge University Press.

Rescher, Nicholas. (1993) "In Matters Religion." In Kelly James Clark (ed.), *Philosophers Who Believe: The Spiritual Journeys of 11 Leading Thinkers.* Downers Grove, IL: InterVarsity Press, pp. 127–36.

Rowe, William. (2007) *Philosophy of Religion: An Introduction,* 4th edition. Belmont, CA: Thomson Wadsworth.

—. (2008) "The Inductive Argument from Evil Against the Existence of God." In Louis P. Pojman and Michael Rea (eds), *Philosophy of Religion: An Anthology,* 5th edition. Belmont, CA: Thomson Wadsworth, pp. 200–7.

Sartre, Jean Paul. (1975) "Existentialism is a Humanism." In Walter Kaufmann (ed.), *Existentialism from Dostoevsky to Sartre.* New York, NY: New American Library, pp. 345–69.

Schellenberg, John L. (1993) *Divine Hiddenness and Human Reason.* Ithaca, NY: Cornell University Press.

—. (2004) "Does Divine Hiddenness Justify Atheism?" In Michael L. Peterson and Raymond J. VanArragon (eds), *Contemporary Debates in Philosophy of Religion.* Malden, MA: Blackwell Publishing, pp. 30–41.

—. (2005) *Prolegomena to a Philosophy of Religion.* Ithaca, NY: Cornell University Press.

—. (2007) *The Wisdom to Doubt: A Justification of Religious Skepticism.* Ithaca, NY: Cornell University Press.

Sessions, William Lad. (2003) "The Certainty of Faith." In Elizabeth S. Radcliffe and Carol J. White (eds), *Faith in Theory and Practice.* Peru, IL: Open Court Publishing, pp. 75–89.

Shermer, Michael. (2011) *The Believing Brain.* New York, NY: Times Books.

Swinburne, Richard. (1979) *The Existence of God.* Oxford: Clarendon Press.

—. (1981) *Faith and Reason.* Oxford: Clarendon Press.

—. (1993) "The Vocation of a Natural Theologian." In Kelly James Clark (ed.), *Philosophers Who Believe: The Spiritual Journeys of 11 Leading Thinkers.* Downers Grove, IL: InterVarsity Press, pp. 179–202.

—. (1996) *Is There A God?* Oxford: Oxford University Press.

Talbott, Thomas. (2004) "No Hell." In Michael L. Peterson and Raymond J. Vanarragon (eds), *Contemporary Debates in Philosophy of Religion.* Malden, MA: Blackwell Publishing, pp. 278–86.

Talioferro, Charles. (1998) *Contemporary Philosophy of Religion.* Malden, MA: Blackwell Publishing.

Tooley, Michael. (1981) "Plantinga's Defense of the Ontological Argument." *Mind* 90: 422–7.

Wainwright, William J. (1994) "Skepticism, Romanticism, and Faith." In Thomas V. Morris (ed.), *God and the Philosophers: The Reconciliation of Faith and Reason*. New York, NY: Oxford University Press, pp. 77–87.

Walton, Douglas. (1997) *Informal Logic: A Pragmatic Approach*. Cambridge: Cambridge University Press.

Wittgenstein, Ludwig. (1967) *Philosophical Investigations*, translated by G. E. M. Anscombe, 3rd edition. Oxford: Blackwell Publishing.

Wykstra, Stephen. (1984) "The Humean Obstacle to Evidential Arguments from Suffering: On Avoiding Evils of 'Appearance.'" *International Journal for Philosophy of Religion* 16: 73–93.

Index

CPSIA information can be obtained at www.ICGtesting.com
Printed in the USA
LVOW04s1658091214

418022LV00013B/371/P